CONTENTS

Welcome to A Conversation Book 1

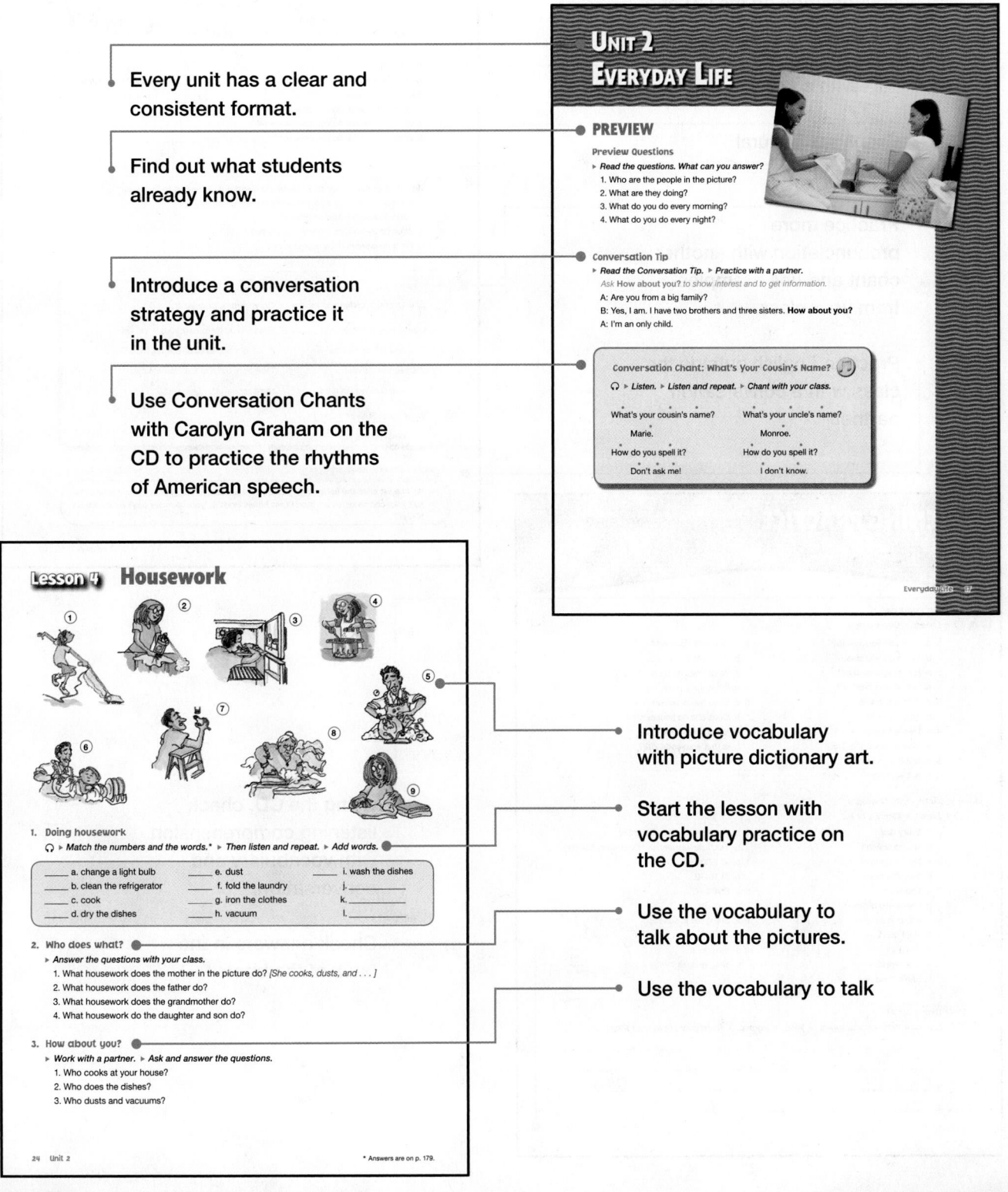

Every unit has a clear and consistent format.

Find out what students already know.

Introduce a conversation strategy and practice it in the unit.

Use Conversation Chants with Carolyn Graham on the CD to practice the rhythms of American speech.

Introduce vocabulary with picture dictionary art.

Start the lesson with vocabulary practice on the CD.

Use the vocabulary to talk about the pictures.

Use the vocabulary to talk

UNIT 2
EVERYDAY LIFE

PREVIEW

Preview Questions
▸ *Read the questions. What can you answer?*
1. Who are the people in the picture?
2. What are they doing?
3. What do you do every morning?
4. What do you do every night?

Conversation Tip
▸ *Read the Conversation Tip.* ▸ *Practice with a partner.*
Ask **How about you?** *to show interest and to get information.*
A: Are you from a big family?
B: Yes, I am. I have two brothers and three sisters. **How about you?**
A: I'm an only child.

Conversation Chant: What's Your Cousin's Name?
⌒ ▸ *Listen.* ▸ *Listen and repeat.* ▸ *Chant with your class.*

What's your cousin's name?   What's your uncle's name?
   Marie.   Monroe.
How do you spell it?   How do you spell it?
   Don't ask me!   I don't know.

Everyday Life 17

Lesson 4 Housework

1. Doing housework
⌒ ▸ *Match the numbers and the words.** ▸ *Then listen and repeat.* ▸ *Add words.*

_____ a. change a light bulb   _____ e. dust   _____ i. wash the dishes
_____ b. clean the refrigerator   _____ f. fold the laundry   j. _____
_____ c. cook   _____ g. iron the clothes   k. _____
_____ d. dry the dishes   _____ h. vacuum   l. _____

2. Who does what?
▸ *Answer the questions with your class.*
1. What housework does the mother in the picture do? *[She cooks, dusts, and . . .]*
2. What housework does the father do?
3. What housework does the grandmother do?
4. What housework do the daughter and son do?

3. How about you?
▸ *Work with a partner.* ▸ *Ask and answer the questions.*
1. Who cooks at your house?
2. Who does the dishes?
3. Who dusts and vacuums?

24   Unit 2   * Answers are on p. 179.

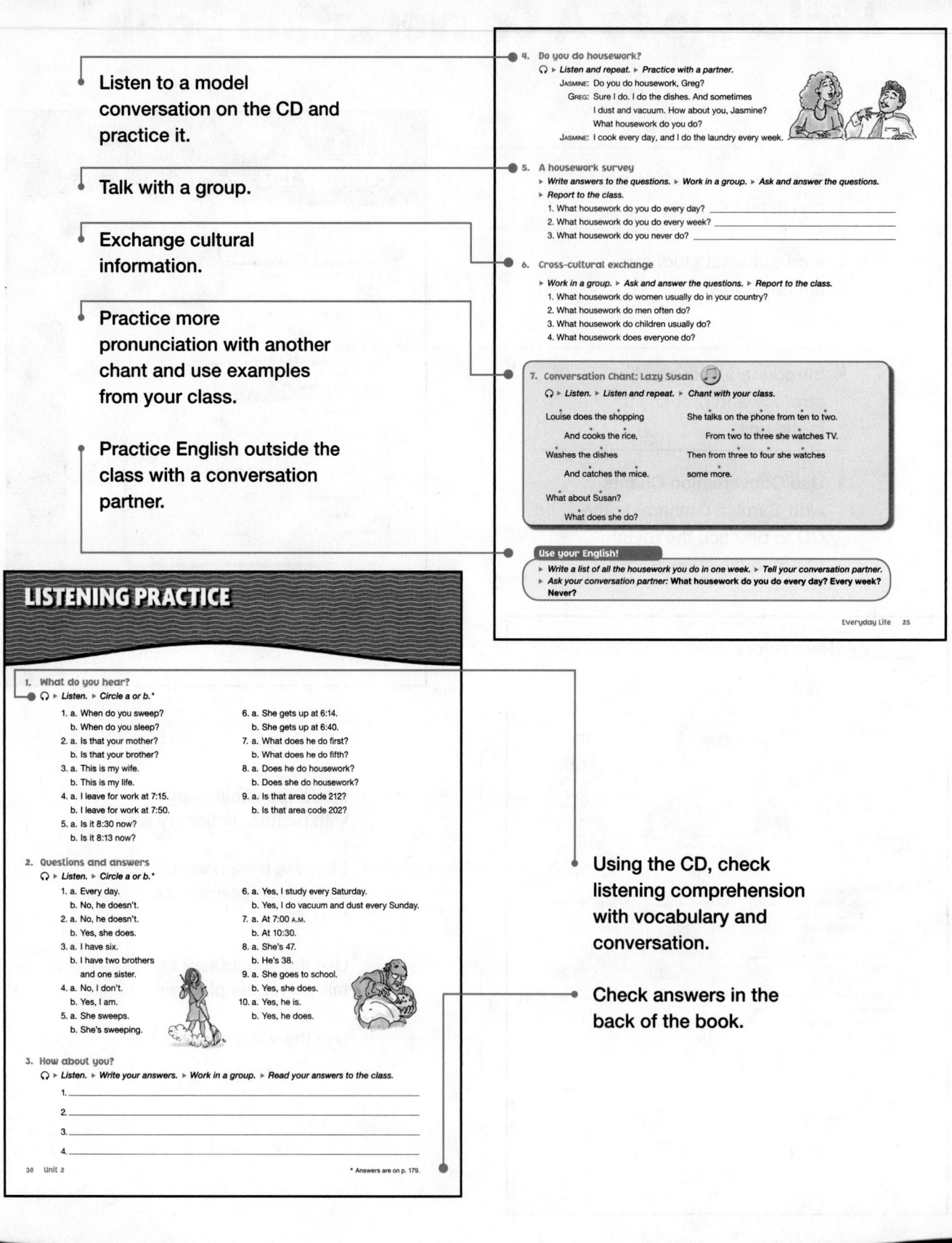

Listen to a model conversation on the CD and practice it.

Talk with a group.

Exchange cultural information.

Practice more pronunciation with another chant and use examples from your class.

Practice English outside the class with a conversation partner.

4. **Do you do housework?**
   ▶ *Listen and repeat.* ▶ *Practice with a partner.*
   JASMINE: Do you do housework, Greg?
   GREG: Sure I do. I do the dishes. And sometimes I dust and vacuum. How about you, Jasmine? What housework do you do?
   JASMINE: I cook every day, and I do the laundry every week.

5. **A housework survey**
   ▶ *Write answers to the questions.* ▶ *Work in a group.* ▶ *Ask and answer the questions.*
   ▶ *Report to the class.*
   1. What housework do you do every day? _____
   2. What housework do you do every week? _____
   3. What housework do you never do? _____

6. **Cross-cultural exchange**
   ▶ *Work in a group.* ▶ *Ask and answer the questions.* ▶ *Report to the class.*
   1. What housework do women usually do in your country?
   2. What housework do men often do?
   3. What housework do children usually do?
   4. What housework does everyone do?

7. **Conversation Chant: Lazy Susan**
   ▶ *Listen.* ▶ *Listen and repeat.* ▶ *Chant with your class.*

   Louise does the shopping
   And cooks the rice,
   Washes the dishes
   And catches the mice.
   What about Susan?
   What does she do?

   She talks on the phone from ten to two.
   From two to three she watches TV.
   Then from three to four she watches
   some more.

   Use your English!
   ▶ *Write a list of all the housework you do in one week.* ▶ *Tell your conversation partner.*
   ▶ *Ask your conversation partner: What housework do you do every day? Every week? Never?*

LISTENING PRACTICE

1. **What do you hear?**
   ▶ *Listen.* ▶ *Circle a or b.*
   1. a. When do you sweep?
      b. When do you sleep?
   2. a. Is that your mother?
      b. Is that your brother?
   3. a. This is my wife.
      b. This is my life.
   4. a. I leave for work at 7:15.
      b. I leave for work at 7:50.
   5. a. Is it 8:30 now?
      b. Is it 8:13 now?
   6. a. She gets up at 6:14.
      b. She gets up at 6:40.
   7. a. What does he do first?
      b. What does he do fifth?
   8. a. Does he do housework?
      b. Does she do housework?
   9. a. Is that area code 212?
      b. Is that area code 202?

2. **Questions and answers**
   ▶ *Listen.* ▶ *Circle a or b.*
   1. a. Every day.
      b. No, he doesn't.
   2. a. No, he doesn't.
      b. Yes, she does.
   3. a. I have six.
      b. I have two brothers and one sister.
   4. a. No, I don't.
      b. Yes, I am.
   5. a. She sweeps.
      b. She's sweeping.
   6. a. Yes, I study every Saturday.
      b. Yes, I do vacuum and dust every Sunday.
   7. a. At 7:00 A.M.
      b. At 10:30.
   8. a. She's 47.
      b. He's 38.
   9. a. She goes to school.
      b. Yes, she does.
   10. a. Yes, he is.
       b. Yes, he does.

3. **How about you?**
   ▶ *Listen.* ▶ *Write your answers.* ▶ *Work in a group.* ▶ *Read your answers to the class.*
   1. _____
   2. _____
   3. _____
   4. _____

Using the CD, check listening comprehension with vocabulary and conversation.

Check answers in the back of the book.

Review the unit with your class.

Play a game—have fun!

1. **Get to know your partner.**
   ▸ *Work with a partner.* ▸ *Ask and answer questions about your families.* ▸ *Take notes.*
   ▸ *Tell the class about your partner.*

2. **What time . . . ?**
   ▸ *Complete the two questions.* ▸ *Write a third question.* ▸ *Walk around your classroom.*
   ▸ *Ask three students your questions.* ▸ *Then answer their questions.*
   1. What time is _____?
   2. What time do _____?
   3. _____?

3. **Housework: Who am I?**
   ▸ *On a piece of paper, write one kind of housework and how often you do it (every day, every week, always, often, sometimes, never).* ▸ *Fold your paper.* ▸ *Make a pile.* ▸ *Open one.*
   ▸ *Read it to the class.* ▸ *Guess who it is.*

4. **What do you do?**
   ▸ *Work with a partner.* ▸ *Ask and answer the questions.*
   1. What do you do first in the morning? Second? Third? Last?
   2. What do you usually do each day of the week?

5. **Favorite day**
   ▸ *Work with a group.* ▸ *Ask and answer the questions.*
   1. What's your favorite day of the week?
   2. Why?

ASSESSMENT

Find out what you have learned.

PART 1: Questions
▸ *Write questions to ask a classmate.*
1. Family: _____
2. Time: _____
3. Morning routine: _____
4. Housework: _____
5. Telephone: _____

PART 2: Speaking
▸ *Work with a partner.* ▸ *Ask and answer your questions from Part 1.*

PART 3: Listening
🎧 ▸ *Listen.* ▸ *Circle a or b.* *

1. a. Yes, she is.
   b. Yes, she does.
2. a. He watches TV.
   b. They practice their English.
3. a. She's 18.
   b. She's fine, thanks.

4. a. It's 6:30. He's getting up.
   b. He gets up and takes a shower.
5. a. Every day.
   b. Yes, I do the dishes.
6. a. I go to work.
   b. I leave for class.

PART 4: Writing
▸ *Write conversations for these pictures.*

HARRY: *What a cute baby!*
GRANDFATHER: *Thanks. She's my* _____
HARRY: *What's her name? How old is she?*
GRANDFATHER: _____

GREG: _____
JASMINE: _____
GREG: _____
JASMINE: _____

* Answers are on p. 179.

SCOPE AND SEQUENCE

Units	Life Skills	Social Language	Conversation Tip	Conversation Chants
UNIT 1 Welcome to Class!	• Making introductions • Spelling names • Practicing cardinal numbers • Talking about countries and continents • Asking and answering questions about colors and clothing • Discussing feelings • Talking about classroom objects, rules, and activities • Giving and following instructions	• Nice to meet you. • Oh, sorry. • Where are you from? • How are you today? • You look good in red. • Where is it? • What's this in English? • Bye. • See you later.	Ask *Is that...?* to confirm new information	• *I'm Worried* • *What's Your First Name?* • *How's Brad?* • *Look at Ted!*
UNIT 2 Everyday Life	• Describing your family • Telling time • Describing daily routines • Talking about housework • Describing your everyday life • Using the telephone	• Are you married? • How many brothers and sisters do you have? • How old are they? • How about you? • What do you do every day? • What time do you get up? • What do you do after class? • Who's calling please? • I'm sorry, you have the wrong number. • Do you have a cell phone?	Ask *How about you?* to show interest and to get information.	• *What's Your Cousin's name?* • *My Dog's a Night Owl!* • *Lazy Susan*
UNIT 3 Your Home	• Describing your home • Talking about kitchens • Talking about dining areas and living rooms • Talking about bedrooms • Talking about bathrooms • Talking about problems at home	• What street do you live on? • What's your apartment number? • What's your ZIP code? • What's your area code? • What's your e-mail address? • What's wrong? • What's the problem? • What do you want to do today? • What do you have to do today?	Ask *How do you say this in English?* and *How do you spell that?* to learn new words.	• *Kathy's Dog Moved to Paris* • *A House Is Not a Home* • *Where's My Toothbrush?*

Listening	CASAS	LAUSD	LCPs
• Answering questions on conversations about greetings, introductions, countries and languages and feelings • Answering questions about classroom items and activities	0.1.1, 0.1.2, 0.1.3, 0.1.4, 0.1.5, 0.1.6, 0.2.1, 0.2.2, 0.2.4, 1.1.9, 1.3.9, 2.2.1, 4.6.1, 5.2.5, 7.4.1, 7.4.7	I.1, I.2, I.4, I.5, I.7, II, II.9 a–d, II.10, II.11.a–c, II.12, II.14. a & b, II.12, II.13, III.A.15, III.A.18, IV.33, IV.34, VIII.58.a–c, VIII.59.a & b	36.04, 39.01, 39.02, 39.03, 39.04, 41.02, 43.02, 45.04, 48.03, 49.01, 49.02, 49.03, 49.17, (56.02)
• Understanding questions and statements about time and everyday life • Understanding and answering questions about everyday life	0.1.1, 0.1.2, 0.1.4, 0.1.5, 0.1.6, 0.2.1, 0.2.2, 0.2.4, 1.4.1, 1.4.7, 1.7.4, 2.1.7, 2.1.8, 2.2.1, 4.6.1, 7.4.1, 7.4.7, 8.1.1, 8.1.2, 8.2.3, 8.2.6	I.3, I.4, I.5, I.6, I.7, II.9.a–d, II.10, II.11.a–c, II.14.a & b, III.B.19 & 20, III.D.25 & 26 & 27, IV.C.38, VII.55, VIII.58.a–c, VIII.59.a & b	36.04, 39.01, 39.02, 39.01, 40.01, 40.02, 42.01, 43.02, 45.08, 49.01, 49.02, 49.03, 49.17
• Listening to questions and answers about addresses and life at home • Answering questions about life at home	0.1.1, 0.1.2, 0.1.4, 0.1.5, 0.1.6, 0.2.1, 0.2.2, 0.2.4, 1.4.1, 1.4.7, 2.2.1, 4.6.1, 7.4.1, 7.4.7, 7.5.5, 8.1.1, 8.1.2, 8.2.2, 8.2.3, 8.2.6	I.7, II.9.a–d, II.10, II.11.a–c, II.14.a & b, IV. C. 38 & 39, VIII. 58. a–c, VIII.59.a & b	36.04, 39.01, 39.02, 41.02, 43.02, 45.08, 49.01, 49.02, 49.03, 49.17

CASAS: Comprehensive Adult Student Assessment System
LAUSD: Los Angeles Unified School District (ESL Beginning Low content standards)
LCPs: Literacy Completion Points (Florida & Texas: Level B Workforce Development Skills & Life Skills)

Units	Life Skills	Social Language	Conversation Tip	Conversation Chants
UNIT 4 Food	• Talking about vegetables • Talking about fruit • Shopping at the supermarket • Talking about breakfast • Talking about lunch • Talking about dinner	• Would you like some more? • Please pass me the bread. • Let's make a salad. • What vegetables do you like? • What's your favorite fruit? • Excuse me, where can I find the milk? • Where do you usually eat lunch? • Who cooks dinner at your house?	Say *please* and *thank you* or *thanks* to be polite.	• *It's Time To Eat!* • *He Likes Cucumbers* • *Let's Eat In*
UNIT 5 Your Community	• Describing your neighborhood and neighbors • Asking directions around town • Using the post office • Using the bank • Calling 911, describing a fire • Calling the police, describing an emergency	• How do you like your neighborhood? • Do you have any problems with your neighbors? • Where's the laundromat? • How do I get to the florist? • Can I help you? • Anything else? • How often do you write letters? • I'd like a stamp. • What do you need to cash a check? • I'm calling to report a fire.	Repeat information to be sure you understand.	• *Nice Neighborhood* • *Lots of Mail* • *Firefighters Climbing*
UNIT 6 Shopping	• Shopping at a mall • Buying shoes • Shopping for clothing • Shopping for jewelry • Understanding sales and advertisements • Shopping in the 21st century	• Where can I get some pencils? • Where do you shop for shoes? • What stores do you recommend? • What size do you wear? • How do they fit? • Can I try it on? • How much is it? • No, thanks. I'm just looking. • What stores have good sales? • Do you like to shop online?	Repeat the question words when you don't understand what someone says.	• *At the Shopping Mall* • *Buying Shoes*
UNIT 7 Your Calendar	• Talking about months, years, and birthdays • Talking about dates and holidays • Understanding weather reports • Talking about good and bad weather • Describing seasons • Taking a trip	• Where were you yesterday? • Will you be home tonight? • When's your birthday? • What do you like to do on your birthday? • What's your favorite holiday? • What's the temperature? • What's the weather like today? • What was it like yesterday? • What kind of weather do you like the most? • Where do you want to go on a trip?	Give extra information when you answer a question.	• *A Surprise Party* • *Sailors Love the Wind* • *Taking a Trip*

Listening	CASAS	LAUSD	LCPs
• Listening to supermarket conversations and completing signs. • Answering questions about meal conversations	0.1.1, 0.1.2, 0.1.4, 0.1.5, 0.1.6, 0.2.1, 0.2.2, 0.2.4, 1.1.3, 1.1.7, 1.2.1, 1.3.1, 1.3.7, 2.2.1, 2.6.4, 4.6.1, 7.4.1, 7.4.7, 8.1.3, 8.2.1	I.7, II.9 a–d, II.10, II.11.a–c, II.14.a & b, VIII.58.a–c, IV.A.31 & 32, IV.B.35 & 36 & 37, VIII.59.a & b	(28.01, 28.03), 39.01, 39.02, 36.04, 41.06, 43.02, 45.03, 49.01, 49.02, 49.03, 49.17
• Answering questions about a post office conversation, an emergency conversation, and a conversation asking directions	0.1.1, 0.1.2, 0.1.4, 0.1.5, 0.1.6, 0.2.1, 0.2.2, 0.2.4, 1.8.1, 1.8.2, 1.9.4, 2.2.1, 2.2.5, 2.5.1, 2.5.2, 2.5.4, 2.6.1, 2.6.3, 4.6.1, 5.6.1, 7.4.1, 7.4.7, 8.3.2	I.7, II.9 a–d, II.10, II.11.a–c, II.14.a & b, III.B.21, III.C.22, III.C.23.a & b, IV.30, VIII.58.a–c, VIII.59.a & b	36.04, 39.01, 39.02, 40.03, 41.09, 42.04, 42.05, 43.02, 43.03, 46.01, 46.02, 49.01, 49.02, 49.03, 49.17
• Choosing answers to shopping questions • Answering questions to place an order	0.1.1, 0.1.2, 0.1.4, 0.1.5, 0.1.6, 0.2.1, 0.2.2, 0.2.4, 1.2.1, 1.2.2, 1.3.1, 1.3.3, 1.3.4, 1.3.5, 1.3.7, 1.3.9, 2.2.1, 2.5.4, 4.6.1, 5.1.6, 7.4.1, 7.4.4, 7.4.7, 8.1.4	I.7, II.9 a–d, II.10, II.11.a–c, II.14.a & b, IV.A.31 & 32 & 33 & 34, VIII.58.a–c, VIII.59.a & b	36.04, 39.01, 39.02, 43.02, 45.01, 45.04, 45.09, 45.10, 49.01, 49.02, 49.03, 49.17
• Choosing answers to holiday questions. • Answering questions about a weather report. • Matching conversations with pictures.	0.1.1, 0.1.2, 0.1.4, 0.1.5, 0.1.6, 0.2.1, 0.2.2, 0.2.4, 1.9.4, 2.2.1, 2.2.3, 2.2.4, 2.2.5, 2.3.2, 2.3.3, 2.6.1, 2.6.3, 2.7.1, 4.6.1, 7.4.1, 7.4.7	I.7, II.9 a–d, II.10, II.11.a–c, II.14.a & b, III.C.23.a & b, III.C.24, III.D.26, III.D.28 & 29, V.40, V.42, VIII.58.a–c, VIII.59.a & b	36.04, 39.01, 39.02, 42.01, 43.01, 43.02, 43.03, 46.04, 47.01, 47.02, 49.01, 49.02, 49.03, 49.17

Units	Life Skills	Social Language	Conversation Tip	Conversation Chants
UNIT 8 **Your Health**	• Staying healthy • Getting sick • Getting medicine at a drugstore • Going to the doctor • Going to the dentist • Going to the hospital	• How are you doing? • What's the matter? • I'm sorry to hear that. • I'm glad to hear that. • I don't feel very well. • What medicine do you recommend? • You should go to the doctor. • Do you like your dentist? • What are the visiting hours? • Where do I check in?	Express your feelings when you hear good news or bad news.	• *What's Wrong with Joe?* • *Exercise Every Day* • *I Like My Dentist.*
UNIT 9 **Your Work**	• Talking about kinds of work • Understanding everyday life at work • Looking for a job • Applying for a job • Discussing safety at work • Leaving a job	• Could you explain that, please? • I didn't get that. • Could you say that again? • What job would you like to have in the future? • What hours do you work? • I'm looking for a job. • Are any companies hiring now? • You need to fill out an application. • What does that sign mean? • He was fired.	Ask for clarification if you don't understand something.	• *A Bad Interview* • *A Day Job or a Night Job?* • *Out of Work*
UNIT 10 **Your Free Time**	• Going out • Talking about your free time • Watching TV and movies • Going to the park • Talking about sports • Discussing future learning plans	• I love to ski. • So do I. • I don't. • Would you like to go to the movies? • That sounds great. • I'm sorry, I can't. • What do you do in your free time? • What kinds of videos do you like? • How often do you go to the park? • What sports are on TV this weekend? • What's your plan for learning more English?	Express agreement and disagreement about what you like.	• *I Love to Fly* • *Free-time Fun* • *The Beautiful Park*

Listening	CASAS	LAUSD	LCPs
• Answering questions about a health conversation and a medical appointment conversation. • Listening to directions in a hospital.	0.1.1, 0.1.2, 0.1.4, 0.1.5, 0.1.6, 0.2.1, 0.2.2, 0.2.4, 2.2.1, 2.5.3, 2.5.4, 3.1.1, 3.1.2, 3.1.3, 3.2.1, 3.3.1, 3.4.1, 3.5.4, 3.5.5, 4.6.1, 7.4.1, 7.4.7	I.7, II.9 a–d, II.10, II.11.a–c, II.14.a & b, III.C. 22. & 23.b, VI.A.44 & 45 & 46, VIII.58.a – c, VIII.59.a & b	24.02, 24.03, 24.04, 36.04, 39.01, 39.02, 43.02, 49.01, 49.02, 49.03, 49.17
• Answering questions on a phone conversation about a want ad • Answering questions on conversations about people's jobs • Listening to questions about jobs and choosing answers	0.1.1, 0.1.2, 0.1.4, 0.1.5, 0.1.6, 0.2.1, 0.2.2, 0.2.4, 2.2.1, 4.1.2, 4.1.3, 4.1.6, 4.1.7, 4.1.8, 4.3.1, 4.3.2, 4.3.3, 4.4.1, 4.4.2, 4.6.1, 4.6.4, 7.4.1, 7.4.7	I.7, II.9 a–d, II.10, II.11.a–c, II.14.a & b, IV.B. 48 & 49, VII.50 & 52 & 53 & 54 & 55 & 56.a & b, VII.57, VIII.58.a-c, VIII.59.a & b	35.01, 35.02, 35.03, 35.04, 35.05, 35.06, 36.01, 36.02, 36.03, 36.04, 36.05, 38.01, 39.01, 39.02, 43.02, 49.01, 49.02, 49.03, 49.17
• Completing a chart based on a free-time conversation • Answering questions about a going-out conversation. • Answering questions about yourself	0.1.1, 0.1.2, 0.1.4, 0.1.5, 0.1.6, 0.2.1, 0.2.2, 0.2.4, 2.2.1, 2.5.5, 2.5.6, 2.6.1, 2.6.2, 2.6.3, 2.7.2, 2.7.5, 2.7.6, 3.5.9, 4.6.1, 5.6.1, 7.4.1, 7.4.4, 7.4.7, 8.3.2	I.7, II.9 a–d, II.10, II.11.a–c, II.14.a & b, III.C.22, VIII.58.a–c, VIII.59.a & b	36.04, 39.01, 39.02, 43.02, 49.01, 49.02, 49.03, 49.17

TO THE TEACHER

Welcome to the Fourth Edition!

Since the first edition of *A Conversation Book*, we have believed that students learn English through their own "lexical" approach—building their vocabulary by talking with one another about topics relevant to their lives. In each edition, we have updated the pedagogy, art, design, topics, and activities. Structure practice has always been, and still is, drawn from the topics, not vice versa. This has made *A Conversation Book* communicative and student centered from the start.

Look who's talking!

The basic principle of *A Conversation Book* has always been for the students to do most of the talking in the class. The teacher takes the role of facilitator and structures the classes, but students' knowledge, experience, and desire to learn are what drive the conversations and the learning. Through a variety of activities, students learn vocabulary and structures as they strive for fluency of expression. And since the topics are familiar to students, they are able to improve their English conversation skills more quickly.

Cross-cultural approach

Learning a foreign language can be threatening and sometimes even overwhelming. We believe that a classroom atmosphere in which differences in backgrounds and belief systems are recognized and valued helps reduce this stress as it enriches the learning experience. To us, a cross-cultural approach is an essential component of English conversation classes, enabling everyone to relax and enjoy the new experiences and new cultural information as they develop the ability to communicate with other English speakers around the world.

Program overview

Due to the flexible nature of the course, *A Conversation Book* can be used in classes from about 50 to 90 hours/semester. Each of the ten units consists of a unit Preview lesson and six two-page topical lessons, followed by one page each of Listening Practice, Review, and Assessment. This design builds schema at the beginning of the unit, develops vocabulary, practices structure in the context of related topics through the six unit lessons, and wraps up each unit with reinforcement and self-assessment.

- **A student audio CD** is provided in the back of some Student Books. It includes the Conversation Chants and Listening Practice .
- **A class audio program CD** is also available with the picture dictionary vocabulary practice and all the model conversations, in addition to the Conversation Chants and Listening Practice.
- **The Teachers' Guide** provides step-by-step instructions on how to implement each lesson, as well as warm-up and expansion activities.

Activities

Among the many activities in the text, these are the backbone of the pedagogy:

- **Preview Questions** introduce the unit topic with questions about a photograph on the Preview page. They help the teacher identify in advance what the students already know and what they need to learn.

- **Conversation Tips** are in the Preview as gambits to help students speak "real" English. They are recycled in the unit and beyond.
- **Conversation Chants** give rhythm and intonation practice with real-life bits of conversation and fun. There are three chants in every unit.
- **Picture Dictionary** activities provide boxed words to study; they are matched to the opening picture, and pronunciation is modeled in the audio program. Students are encouraged to add words to the word list.
- **Model conversations** include contextualized formulaic expressions and vocabulary about the topic. The audio program provides the listening component for each of these brief conversations.
- **How about you?** activities give partners opportunities to interview each other, converting the model conversations into conversations about themselves.
- **Cross-cultural exchanges** encourage students to compare and contrast cultures, fostering an appreciation of the richness of the class' experiences and the diversity of the cultures of English speakers.
- **Games** add a light touch—and fun—while learning.
- **Use your English!** activities get students outside the classroom—talking about life, finding out about their community, or doing Internet activities.

Acknowledgments

Our thanks to colleagues and friends who have worked on this project with us: Carolyn Graham, our new co-author; Sarah Lynn, who has joined us in the writing of this new edition; Laura Le Dréan, our editor at Longman; Karen Davy, our development editor; Robert Ruvo, our production editor, and Shana McGuire, editorial assistant. Most of all, our thanks to Gene and Munchi for their endless patience.

Tina Carver and Sandi Fotinos-Riggs

🎵 A NOTE FROM CAROLYN GRAHAM

What is a jazz chant?

A jazz chant is a rhythmic expression of natural spoken American English. It is not a distortion of the spoken form. It simply draws attention to the powerful rhythm that is present in the natural speech of a native speaker of American English.

The rhythm is the very simple **one, two, three, four** that is found in early traditional American jazz and flows right into the most modern sounds of hip-hop and rap. Jazz chanting is not rapping, however. There is a very important distinction. Rapping is a poetic distortion of the language but is not meant to sound like a natural conversation. *Jazz chanting is an exact reproduction of the natural speech pattern*. I found all of my best jazz chants simply by carefully listening to the language I heard around me at home and on the streets of New York City.

What is a conversation chant?

A conversation chant is simply a jazz chant written for two or more voices. You will see that many of my chants in this book use a simple question-response pattern to reinforce and expand on the material introduced in each unit.

For example, in Unit 1, Lesson 3 people ask one another how they are and answer with different vocabulary, both positive (*fine, happy, great*) and negative (*not so great, tired,* etc.). In my chant "*How's Brad?*" I use words introduced in the unit under *Feelings* (*sad, mad, confused, excited, worried, happy*) and add rhyming words to help students hear and learn the sounds: *How's Brad? He's very sad. How's Tad? He's very mad.* I want the students to hear

the *Brad/sad- Tad/mad* rhyming pattern. This chant also offers practice in the sound of the contractions (*How's, He's, Jack's, I'm, They're, We're*), the negative pattern with "*not*" (*I'm not sad I'm not mad*), and the use of "*so*" (*so is Sue*).

In Unit 7, Lesson 6, I offer a *Yes/No question, short*-response chant moving from present to past and back to present, using the verb *be* and other verbs (*Are you ready to go? Yes, I am. Did you pack your sunhat? Yes, I did. Are your bags all packed? Yes, they are.*) Now I bring in an information question and answer. (*Where's your computer? It's in the car.*) This gives a nice opportunity to practice the contrasting intonation pattern of the rising *Yes/No* question and the falling information question. This chant also includes singular/plural contrasts (it/they). Conversation chants like these constantly reinforce grammar, vocabulary, stress, and intonation.

I was very pleased when my friends Sandi Fotinos-Riggs and Tina Carver invited me to contribute some chants to the new edition of their wonderful book. The chants wrote themselves. This happens when the basic material is really good. When I say "really good," what I mean is *Is this real language? Is it useful and appropriate for the age of the student we are teaching? Will it bring some joy into the language classroom?* I hope and believe that the answers are all **yes**. The conversation chants in this book are meant to offer a fun way to practice the sounds of English, reinforce basic grammar patterns, and build conversational vocabulary. I hope you and your students will enjoy chanting them as much as I enjoyed writing them.

Carolyn Graham

UNIT 1
WELCOME TO CLASS!

PREVIEW

Preview Questions

▶ *Read the questions. What can you answer?*

1. What do you see in the picture?
   Who do you see?
2. What's happening in the picture?
3. What are the people saying?
4. How are you today?

Conversation Tip

▶ *Read the Conversation Tip.* ▶ *Practice with a partner.*

Ask **Is that _____ ?** *to confirm new information.*

A: My name's Keiko.
B: Sorry. **Is that Keiko?**
A: Yes, that's right.

Conversation Chant: I'm Worried

🎧 ▶ *Listen.* ▶ *Listen and repeat.* ▶ *Chant with your class.*

I'm worried.

So are they.

They're very worried.

So is Ray.

He's very worried.

So is Sky.

She's worried to death!

So am I!

Lesson 1 Introductions

1. Introductions

🎧 ▶ *Match the numbers and the words.** ▶ *Then listen and repeat.* ▶ *Add words.*

_____ a. making a name tag	_____ d. smiling	g. _____
_____ b. shaking hands	_____ e. talking	
_____ c. showing a name tag	f. _____	

2. What are they doing?

▶ *Answer the questions with your class.*

1. What are Paco and Keiko doing?

2. What are Maria and Tom doing?

3. Who is talking?

4. Who is smiling?

3. What are they saying?

🎧 ▶ *Listen and repeat.* ▶ *Practice with a partner.*

1. PACO: Hi. I'm Paco.

   KEIKO: Nice to meet you, Paco. My name's Keiko.

   PACO: Sorry. Is that Keiko?

   KEIKO: Yes, that's right.

   PACO: Nice to meet you, too, Keiko.

2. MARIA: Hello. My name's Maria.

   TOM: Nice to meet you, Maria. I'm Tom.

   MARIA: Hi, Don. Nice to meet you.

   TOM: No, it's not Don. It's Tom.

   MARIA: Oh, sorry. Nice to meet you, Tom.

* Answers are on p. 179.

4. Meet your group!

► *Make a name tag.* ► *Work in a group.* ► *Introduce yourselves.*

5. Conversation Chant: What's Your First Name?

🎧 ► *Listen.* ► *Listen and repeat.* ► *Chant with your class.* ► *Repeat with your classmates' names.*

What's your first name?

Sandy

How do you spell Sandy?

S—a—ndy

How do you pronounce it?

Sandy

6. How many?

► *Review NUMBERS on page 169.* ► *Work in a group.* ► *Ask the questions and fill in the chart.* ► *Compare your numbers with the class.*

1. How many men are in your class? _____

2. How many women are in your class? _____

3. How many classmates have long hair ? _____

4. How many classmates have short hair ? _____

5. How many classmates have glasses  ? _____

7. See you later

🎧 ► *Listen and repeat.* ► *Say good-bye to all your classmates.*

JOE: Bye, Bill.

BILL: See you later, Joe.

KATIE: Have a good day, Joe.

JOE: You, too, Katie. Good-bye.

Use your English!

► *Say hello to five people outside your classroom.* ► *Find a conversation partner: an e-pal, a phone pal, or a friend.* ► *Write your conversation partner's name here* _____.

Lesson 2 Countries

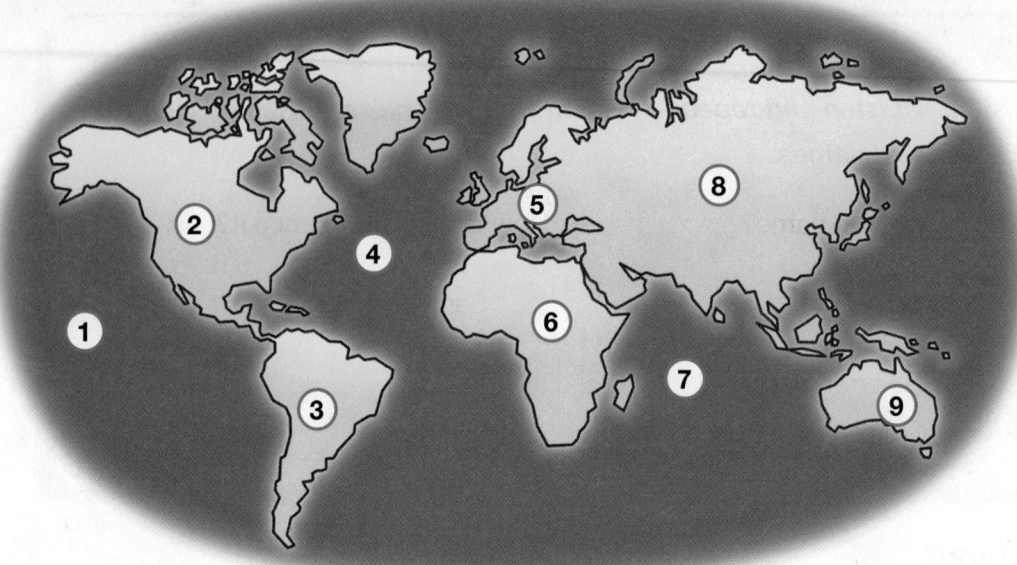

1. Map of the World

🎧 ▸ *Match the numbers and the words.** ▸ *Then listen and repeat.* ▸ *Add words.*

_____ a. Africa	_____ e. Europe	_____ i. South America
_____ b. Asia	_____ f. Indian Ocean	j. _____
_____ c. Atlantic Ocean	_____ g. North America	k. _____
_____ d. Australia	_____ h. Pacific Ocean	l. _____

2. What's on the map?

▸ *Answer the questions with your class.*

1. What are the oceans? *[The Atlantic Ocean, the _____]*

2. What are the continents? *[Asia, _____]*

3. Where are you from? Draw a circle on the map.

4. Where are you now? Draw an X on the map.

3. Where is she from?

🎧 ▸ *Put the conversation in order.* ▸ *Number the sentences from 1 to 6.* ▸ *Then listen and repeat.* ▸ *Practice with a partner.*

_____ Mɪᴀ: No, it's in South America.

_____ Aʟᴇx: What language do you speak?

_____ Mɪᴀ: I'm from Venezuela.

_____ Mɪᴀ: Spanish.

_____ Aʟᴇx: Venezuela? Is that in Central America?

_____ Aʟᴇx: Where are you from?

* Answers are on p. 179.

4. Where are you from?

▶ *Write answers to the questions.* ▶ *Ask and answer the questions with a partner.*
Tell the class about your partner.

1. What's your name? _____

2. Where are you from? _____

3. Where is your country? _____

4. What language do people speak in your country?_____

5. Where in the world is that country?

▶ **Look at the maps on pages 161-168.** ▶ **Answer the questions with your class.**

6. What's the country?

▶ *Think.*

▶ *Write two sentences about a country.*

▶ *Fold your paper.*

▶ *Make a pile.*

▶ *Open one.*
Read it to the class.

▶ *What's the country?*
Guess.

Use your English!

▶ *Tell your conversation partner about your country.* ▶ *Answer these questions:* **Where are you from? Where is your country? What language(s) do people speak there?** ▶ *Ask your conversation partner about his or her country.*

Lesson 3 Feelings

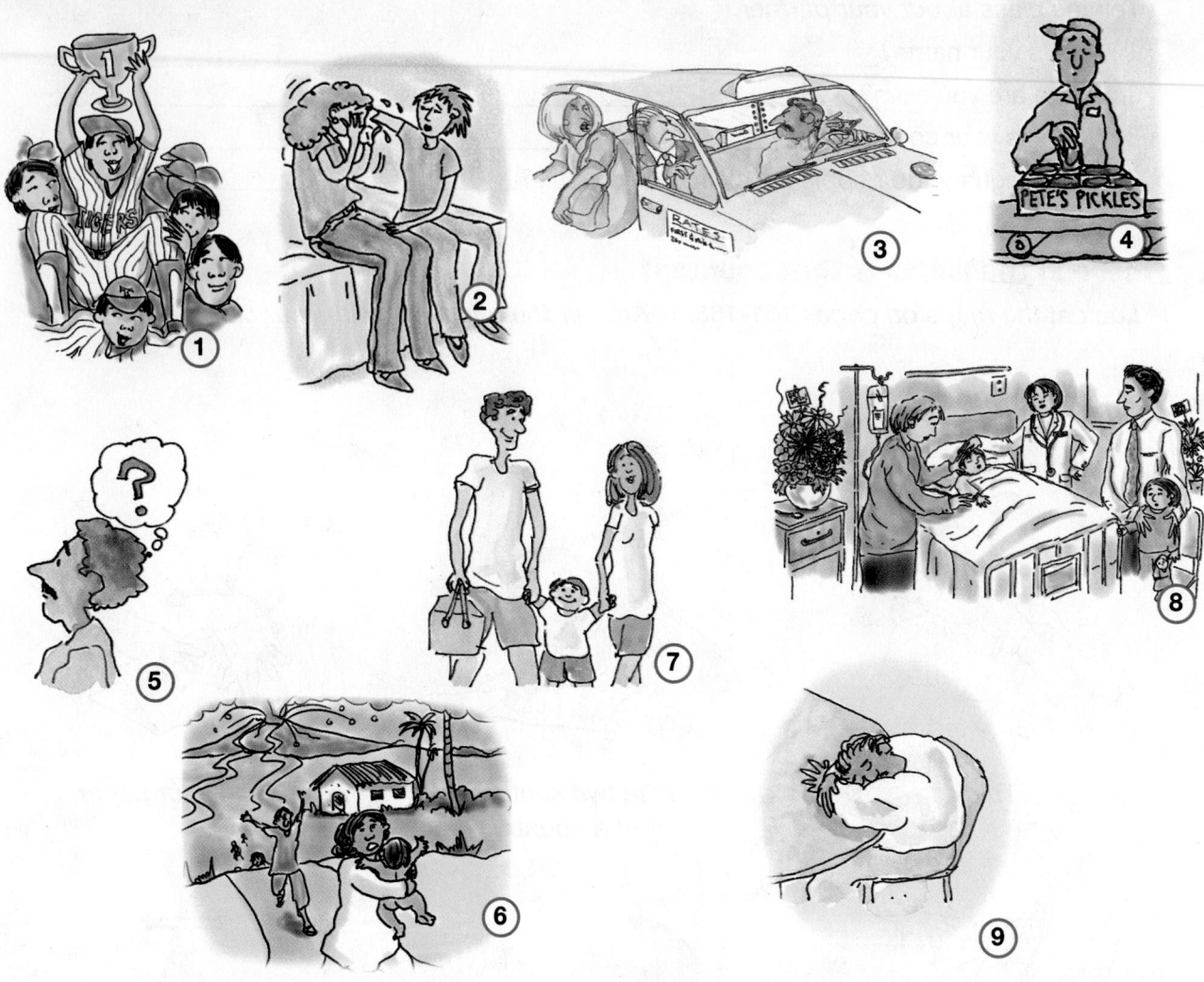

1. Feelings

🎧 ▸ *Match the numbers and the words.** ▸ Then listen and repeat. ▸ Add words.*

_____ a. afraid	_____ e. excited	_____ i. worried
_____ b. angry (mad)	_____ f. happy	j. _____
_____ c. bored	_____ g. sad	k. _____
_____ d. confused	_____ h. tired	l. _____

2. How are they?

▸ **Answer the questions with your class.**

1. How are these people feeling?

2. Are you feeling like one of these people today? Which one?

    * Answers are on p. 179.

3. How are you today?

🎧 ▸ *Listen and repeat.* ▸ *Practice with a partner.*

LISA: Hi, Kevin! How are you today?

KEVIN: I'm fine, thanks, Lisa.

LISA: How's your English class?

KEVIN: My class is great. I'm excited!

LISA: Oh, that's wonderful.

KEVIN: And how about you, Lisa? How are you?

LISA: Not so great.

KEVIN: Not so great? What's the matter?

LISA: I'm tired today.

KEVIN: Oh, I'm sorry.

4. How are your classmates today?

▸ *Ask four classmates:* **How are you today?** *and* **How's your English class?**

▸ *Report to the class.*

5. Conversation Chant: How's Brad?

🎧 ▸ *Listen.* ▸ *Listen and repeat.* ▸ *Chant with your class.*

How's Brad?

He's very sad.

How's Tad?

He's very mad!

Jack's confused,

So is Sue.

I'm excited!

How about you?

I'm happy. I'm not sad.

I'm happy. I'm not mad.

They're very worried.

He's very mad.

But we're very happy.

We're not sad.

6. How am I feeling?

▸ *Work in a group.* ▸ *Act out a feeling.* ▸ *Ask:* **How am I feeling?** ▸ *Have the group guess.*

Use your English!

▸ *Ask your conversation partner and two more people:* **How are you today?**

Lesson 4 Clothes and Colors

1. Clothes

🎧 ▶ *Match the numbers and the words.* * ▶ *Then listen and repeat.* ▶ *Add words.*

One		Pair of	
_____ a. blouse	_____ e. suit	_____ h. jeans	_____ l. shorts
_____ b. dress	_____ f. sweater	_____ i. pants	_____ m. socks
_____ c. shirt	_____ g. T-shirt	_____ j. sandals	n. _____
_____ d. skirt		_____ k. shoes	

2. Colors

▶ *Answer the questions with your class.*

1. What colors are the clothes in the pictures?

   [The dress is blue. The pants are brown.]

2. What colors are your classmates wearing today?

   [Kate's wearing green.]

3. What clothes are your classmates wearing?

   [Ted's wearing shorts and a T-shirt.]

4. What's your favorite color?

* Answers are on p. 179.

3. True or false?

▶ *Work in a group.* ▶ *Take turns: Tell your group something TRUE or FALSE about your clothes.* ▶ *Your group says:* **Yes, that's true** *or* **No, that's false**.

A: I'm wearing a purple sweatshirt.
B: Yes, that's true. You're wearing a purple sweatshirt.

A: I'm wearing a yellow dress.
B: No, that's false. You're not wearing a dress. You're wearing jeans.

4. Conversation Chant: Look at Ted!

🎧 ▶ *Listen.* ▶ *Listen and repeat.* ▶ *Chant with your class.*

Look at Ted! What's he wearing?

Shorts and a T-shirt,

Bright red!

Ted looks good in red. WOW!

Ted looks good in red.

Look at Kate! What's she wearing?

Pants and a sweatshirt,

Dark green.

Kate looks great in green. WOW!

Kate looks great in green!

Look at Sue! What's she wearing?

Sue's in blue,

Baby blue.

Sue looks fine in blue. WOW!

Sue looks fine in blue.

So do you!

5. You look great in black!

▶ *Tell four classmates:* **I like your _____. You look great in _____.**
                                          (clothes)   *(color)*

Use your English!

▶ *Tell two people:* **I like your _____. You look good in _____.**
                                    (clothes)   *(color)*

▶ *Ask your conversation partner about clothes and colors.* ▶ *Ask:* **What are you wearing today? What colors are your clothes? What's your favorite color?**

Lesson 5   In Your Classroom

1. The classroom

🎧 ▸ *Match the numbers and the words.** ▸ *Then listen and repeat.* ▸ *Add words.*

_____ a. a board	_____ g. a door	_____ m. a pencil
_____ b. a book	_____ h. an eraser	_____ n. a wastebasket
_____ c. a chair	_____ i. a map	_____ o. a window
_____ d. chalk	_____ j. a notebook	p. _____
_____ e. a clock	_____ k. paper	q. _____
_____ f. a desk	_____ l. a pen	r. _____

2. What's in the classroom?

▸ *Answer the questions with your class.*

1. What's in this picture? *[There's a door. There are books.]*

2. What colors are the things in the picture? *[The door's green. The books are . . .]*

3. How many _____ are there in the picture? *[There's one door. There are four books.]*

4. How many _____ are there in your classroom? *[There are . . . There's one . . .]*

       * Answers are on p. 179.

3. What's that in English?

🎧 ▸ *Listen and repeat.* ▸ *Work in a group.* ▸ *Ask and answer* **What's that in English?** *about your classroom.* ▸ *Write a class list of new words in English.*

SUE: What's that in English, Oscar?

OSCAR: I don't know. Let's ask the teacher.

SUE: What's that in English, please?

TEACHER: It's a map.

SUE: A map?

TEACHER: That's right. M-a-p. Map.

SUE: Thank you.

4. Where is it?

🎧 ▸ *Listen and repeat.* ▸ *Work with a partner.* ▸ *Add two more questions and answers about the picture.* ▸ *Work in a group.* ▸ *Ask and answer your questions.*

1. Where's the wastebasket?
   It's **next to** the desk.

2. Where are the students?
   They're **in** the classroom.

3. Where's the map?
   It's **in front of** the board.

4. Where's the board?
   It's **behind** the map.

5. Where are the books?
   They're **on** a desk.

6. Where's the globe?
   It's **under** the window.

7. Where's the _____?
   It's _____ .

8. Where are the _____?
   They're _____ .

5. Your classroom

▸ *Work in a group.* ▸ *Write four* **Where** *questions about your classroom.* ▸ *Read your questions to the class.* ▸ *Have your classmates answer the questions.*

6. What is it?

▸ *Work in a group.* ▸ *Think about a thing in your classroom—don't say it! Have your group ask* **YES/NO** *questions and guess the thing.*

Use your English!

▸ *Tell your conversation partner about your classroom.*

Lesson 6 Taking a Break

1. Actions

🎧 ▶ *Match the numbers and the words.** ▶ *Then listen and repeat.* ▶ *Add words.*

_____ a. coming in	_____ g. pointing	_____ m. waving
_____ b. crying	_____ h. reading	_____ n. yawning
_____ c. drawing	_____ i. sitting	o. _____
_____ d. drinking	_____ j. sleeping	p. _____
_____ e. erasing	_____ k. standing	q. _____
_____ f. laughing	_____ l. walking	

2. What are they doing?

▶ *Answer the questions with your class.*

1. This class is taking a break. What are the students doing?

   [Student 2 is erasing the board. Many students are sitting. Student 1 is…]

2. What are the students in your class doing now?

3. What is your teacher doing now?

* Answers are on p. 179.

3. What am I doing?

🎧 ▸ *Listen and repeat.* ▸ *Work in a group.* ▸ *Act out an activity.* ▸ *Ask:* **What am I doing?**
▸ *Your group guesses the activity.*

A: What am I doing?
B: You're laughing.
A: No, I'm not laughing. I'm smiling.

A: What am I doing?
B: You're crying.
A: You're right! I'm crying! It's your turn now.

4. Follow instructions.

🎧 ▸ *Listen and repeat.* ▸ *Work in a group.* ▸ *Add two instructions.* ▸ *Give and follow the instructions.*

1. Stand up.
2. Say hello.
3. Wave.
4. Don't wave.
5. Smile.

6. Don't smile.
7. Laugh!
8. Sit down.
9. _____
10. _____

5. Class rules

▸ *Work in a group.* ▸ *Write rules for your class.* ▸ *Read your rules to the class.* ▸ *Make a list of class rules on the board.*

DO	DON'T
1. Listen to the teacher.	1. Don't sleep in class.
2. _____	2. _____
3. _____	3. _____

Use your English!

▸ *Ask two people:* **What are you doing right now?** ▸ *Tell your conversation partner about your class.*

LISTENING PRACTICE

1. What do you hear?

🎧 ▶ *Listen.* ▶ *Circle a or b.* *

1. a. What's her name?
   b. What's his name?

2. a. What's he doing?
   b. What's she doing?

3. a. Where are they from?
   b. Where are you from?

4. a. What color is that shirt?
   b. What color is that skirt?

5. a. Blue is my favorite color.
   b. Black is my favorite color.

6. a. What are you drawing?
   b. What are you drinking?

7. a. I'm so sad!
   b. I'm so mad!

8. a. Wear your gray T-shirt.
   b. Don't wear your gray T-shirt.

2. Questions and answers

🎧 ▶ *Listen.* ▶ *Circle a or b.* *

1. a. It's an eraser.
   b. Yes, it's in English.

2. a. We're writing on the board.
   b. They're reading.

3. a. I'm tired.
   b. Yes, I am.

4. a. Black pants and a white shirt.
   b. He's bored.

5. a. It's green.
   b. They're blue.

6. a. They're on my desk.
   b. It's under the table.

7. a. His name is Mario.
   b. Her name is Marie.

8. a. It's in Europe.
   b. I'm from Europe.

3. About you

🎧 ▶ *Listen.* ▶ *Write your answers.* ▶ *Work in a group.* ▶ *Read your answers to the class.*

1. _____

2. _____

3. _____

* Answers are on p. 179.

REVIEW

1. **Get to know your partner**
    - ▶ *Work with a partner.* ▶ *Ask and answer the questions.* ▶ *Write your partner's answers.*
    - ▶ *Tell the class about your partner.*
        1. What's your name? _____
        2. Where are you from? _____
        3. What languages do you speak? _____
        4. How are you today? _____
        5. What's your favorite color? _____

2. **What's your partner wearing?**
    - ▶ *Work with a partner.* ▶ *Look at your partner's clothes.* ▶ *Sit back-to-back.* ▶ *What's your partner wearing? Say:* **You're wearing . . .**

3. **Who am I?**
    - ▶ *Write a description of yourself on a piece of paper.* [I'm a (man/woman). My hair is . . . I'm wearing . . .] ▶ *Fold your paper.* ▶ *Make a pile.* ▶ *Open one.* ▶ *Read it to the class.*
    - ▶ *Guess who it is.*

4. **What's in your classroom?**
    - ▶ *Work in a group.* ▶ *List ten things in your classroom.* ▶ *Share your ideas with the class.*
    - ▶ *Write a class list on the board.*

5. **Question practice**
    - ▶ *Write two questions from each lesson in this unit.* ▶ *Work with a partner.* ▶ *Ask and answer the questions.*

        Lesson 1: _____

        Lesson 2: _____

        Lesson 3: _____

        Lesson 4: _____

        Lesson 5: _____

        Lesson 6: _____

ASSESSMENT

PART 1: Questions

▶ *Write questions to ask a classmate.*

1. Introductions: _____

2. Countries: _____

3. Feelings: _____

4. Clothes: _____

5. Colors: _____

6. Your classroom: _____

7. Actions: _____

PART 2: Speaking

▶ *Work with a partner.* ▶ *Ask and answer your questions from Part 1.*

PART 3: Listening

🎧 ▶ *Listen.* ▶ *Circle a or b.* *

1. a. My name's Ed.
   b. I'm fine, thanks.

2. a. A T-shirt.
   b. I'm smiling.

3. a. I'm from Mexico.
   b. I feel fine, thanks.

4. a. It's my pen.
   b. Yellow.

5. a. He's tired today.
   b. She's standing at the board.

6. a. It's on the desk.
   b. I'm answering questions.

PART 4: Writing

▶ *Write conversations for these pictures.*

MAC: _____

JACK: _____

MAC: _____

JACK: _____

JILL: _____

PHIL: _____

JILL: _____

* Answers are on p. 179.

UNIT 2
EVERYDAY LIFE

PREVIEW

Preview Questions

▶ *Read the questions. What can you answer?*

1. Who are the people in the picture?
2. What are they doing?
3. What do you do every morning?
4. What do you do every night?

Conversation Tip

▶ *Read the Conversation Tip.* ▶ *Practice with a partner.*

Ask **How about you?** *to show interest and to get information.*

A: Are you from a big family?

B: Yes, I am. I have two brothers and three sisters. **How about you?**

A: I'm an only child.

Conversation Chant: What's Your Cousin's Name?

🎧 ▶ *Listen.* ▶ *Listen and repeat.* ▶ *Chant with your class.*

What's your cousin's name?

Marie.

How do you spell it?

Don't ask me!

What's your uncle's name?

Monroe.

How do you spell it?

I don't know.

Lesson 1   Your Family

1. Family pictures

🎧 ▸ *Match the numbers and the words.* ▸ *Use some numbers more than once.* *

▸ *Then listen and repeat.* ▸ *Add words.*

_____ a. boy   _____ e. father   _____ i. mother   _____ m. wife

_____ b. brother   _____ f. girl   _____ j. parents   n. _____

_____ c. children   _____ g. husband   _____ k. sister   o. _____

_____ d. daughter   _____ h. married couple _____ l. son

2. That's me.

🎧 ▸ *Listen and repeat.* ▸ *Practice with a partner.*

DONALD: Look at my family pictures. That's my wife, Laura,
         and me in the first picture.

HARRY: Your wife is pretty.

DONALD: Thank you. And these are my two children. The girl is
         my daughter, Becky, and the boy is my son, Ben.

HARRY: How old are they?

DONALD: Ben is eleven years old, and Becky's eight.

HARRY: You have a wonderful family, Donald.

3. Who are they?

▸ *Answer the questions with your class.*

1. Who's the woman in Donald's family pictures?

2. Who's the man?

3. Who are the boy and girl?

* Answers are on p. 179.

4. Your family

▶ *Work with a partner.* ▶ *Ask and answer the questions.* ▶ *Tell the class about your family or your partner's family.*

1. How many brothers and sisters do you have? What are their names? How old are they?

2. Are you married?

3. Do you have any children? What are their names? How old are they?

4. What are your parents' names?

5. More family pictures

🎧 ▶ *Match the numbers and the words.** ▶ *Then listen and repeat.* ▶ *Add words.*

_____ a. aunt

_____ b. cat

_____ c. cousin

_____ d. dog

_____ e. grandfather

_____ f. grandmother

_____ g. grandparents

_____ h. nephew

_____ i. niece

_____ j. uncle

k. _____

6. How about you?

▶ *Work in a group.* ▶ *Ask and answer the questions.*

1. How many aunts and uncles do you have? _____

2. How many nephews and nieces do you have? _____

3. How many cousins do you have? _____

4. Do you have a dog? _____ A cat?_____

Use your English!

▶ *Tell your family about your English class.* ▶ *Bring pictures of your family to class.* ▶ *Show your pictures and tell about your family.*

Lesson 2 Time

1. wake up
2. have breakfast
3. go to class
4. have lunch
5. do homework
6. have dinner
7. go to bed
8. sleep

1. Time

🎧 ▶ *Match the numbers and the words.** ▶ *Then listen and repeat.* ▶ *Add words.*

_____ a. eight-thirty A.M.	_____ d. noon	_____ g. six forty-five P.M.
_____ b. four P.M.	_____ e. seven-fifteen A.M.	_____ h. ten-thirty P.M.
_____ c. midnight	_____ f. six A.M.	i. _____

2. A student's day

▶ *Answer the questions with your class.*

1. What does the student do every day? *[He wakes up. He has breakfast. . . .]*
2. What time does he have breakfast, lunch, and dinner? *[He has breakfast at. . . .]*
3. How many hours does he sleep every night? *[He sleeps . . .]*

3. How about you?

▶ *Work with a partner.* ▶ *Ask and answer the questions.*

1. How many hours do you sleep every night? *[I sleep . . .]*
2. What time do you wake up in the morning? *[I wake up at . . .]*
3. What time do you go to bed at night? *[I go to bed at . . .]*
4. What time do you have breakfast, lunch, and dinner? *[I have . . .]*
5. What time do you do homework? *[I do homework at . . .]*

   * Answers are on p. 179.

4. Are you an early bird or a night owl?

🎧 ▸ *Listen and repeat.* ▸ *Practice with a partner.*

LENA: Are you an early bird, Jeff? Or are you a night owl?

JEFF: I'm an early bird. I get up at six every morning.
How about you?

LENA: I'm a night owl. I go to bed at one or two A.M.
and wake up around ten.

JEFF: At ten? My first class is at eight. What time do you go to class?

LENA: My English class is at eleven, but I'm not always on time.
Some days I'm late.

5. A sleep survey

▸ *Work in a group.* ▸ *Ask and answer the questions.* ▸ *How many said YES? How many said NO?* ▸ *Count your group's answers.* ▸ *Write the numbers in the chart and report to the class.*

QUESTIONS	YES	NO
1. Do you get up early in the morning?	☐	☐
2. Do you go to bed late?	☐	☐
3. Do you sleep eight hours every night?	☐	☐
4. Do you have an alarm clock?	☐	☐
5. Are you on time to class every day?	☐	☐
6. Do you sometimes wake up after noon?	☐	☐

6. Conversation Chant: My Dog's a Night Owl!

🎧 ▸ *Listen.* ▸ *Listen and repeat.* ▸ *Chant with your class.*

My dog's a night owl!

   He loves to stay up late.

He never gets up early.

   He's always asleep at eight.

My cat's an early bird!

   She wakes up with the sun.

She wakes me up at six o'clock.

   For her that's lots of fun.

Use your English!

▸ *Ask your conversation partner questions from this lesson.*

Lesson 3   Morning Routines

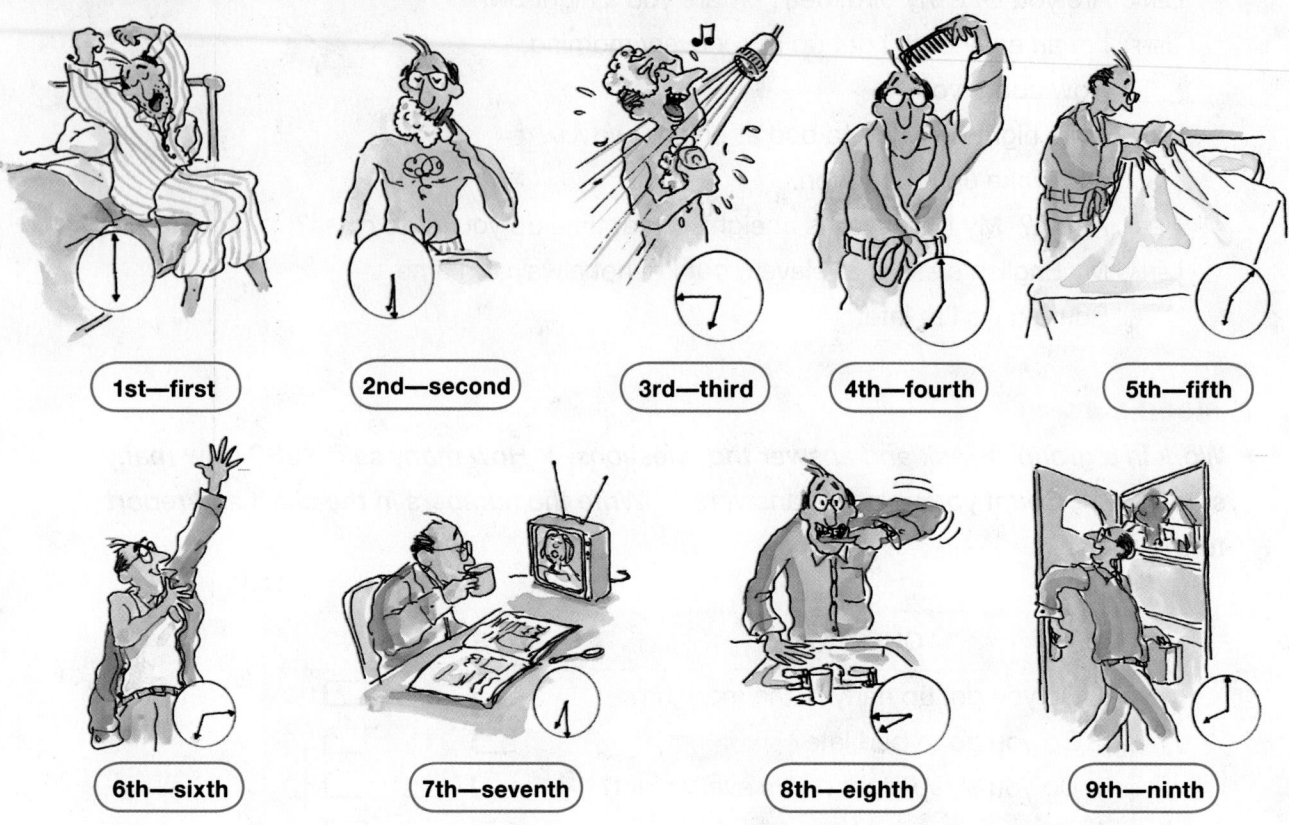

1st—first   2nd—second   3rd—third   4th—fourth   5th—fifth

6th—sixth   7th—seventh   8th—eighth   9th—ninth

1. A morning routine

🎧 ▸ *Match the numbers and the words.** ▸ *Then listen and repeat.* ▸ *Add words.*

_____ a. brush his teeth	_____ f. leave for work	_____ k. watch the news
_____ b. comb his hair	_____ g. make his bed	l. _____
_____ c. get dressed	_____ h. read the newspaper	m. _____
_____ d. get up	_____ i. shave	
_____ e. have a cup of coffee	_____ j. take a shower	

2. First, next, last

▸ *Answer the questions with your class.*

1. What does Ed do first every morning? *[First, he gets up.]* What does he do next?
   [Next, he…]

2. What does Ed do third? Fourth? Fifth? Sixth? Seventh? Eighth? What does he do last?
   [Last, he . . .]

3. Describe Ed's morning routine with the times. *[At six A.M., he gets up. . . .]*

* Answers are on p. 179.

3. How about you?

▸ *Work with a partner.* ▸ *Describe your morning routine.* [*First, I get up. Next, I . . .*]

4. Find someone who . . .

▸ *Talk to your classmates.* ▸ *Ask the questions.*

▸ *Write names to complete the sentences.*

▸ *Report to the class.*

1. _____ sings in the shower.
2. _____ watches TV in the morning.
3. _____ has coffee in the morning.
4. _____ reads a newspaper in the morning.
5. _____ makes the bed every morning.

5. What am I doing?

▸ *Work in a group.* ▸ *Act out an activity from your morning routine.* ▸ *Ask* **What am I doing?**

▸ *The group guesses the activity.*

Use your English!

▸ *Ask your conversation partner:* **What do you do in the morning?**

▸ *Learn a song in English.*

Lesson 4   Housework

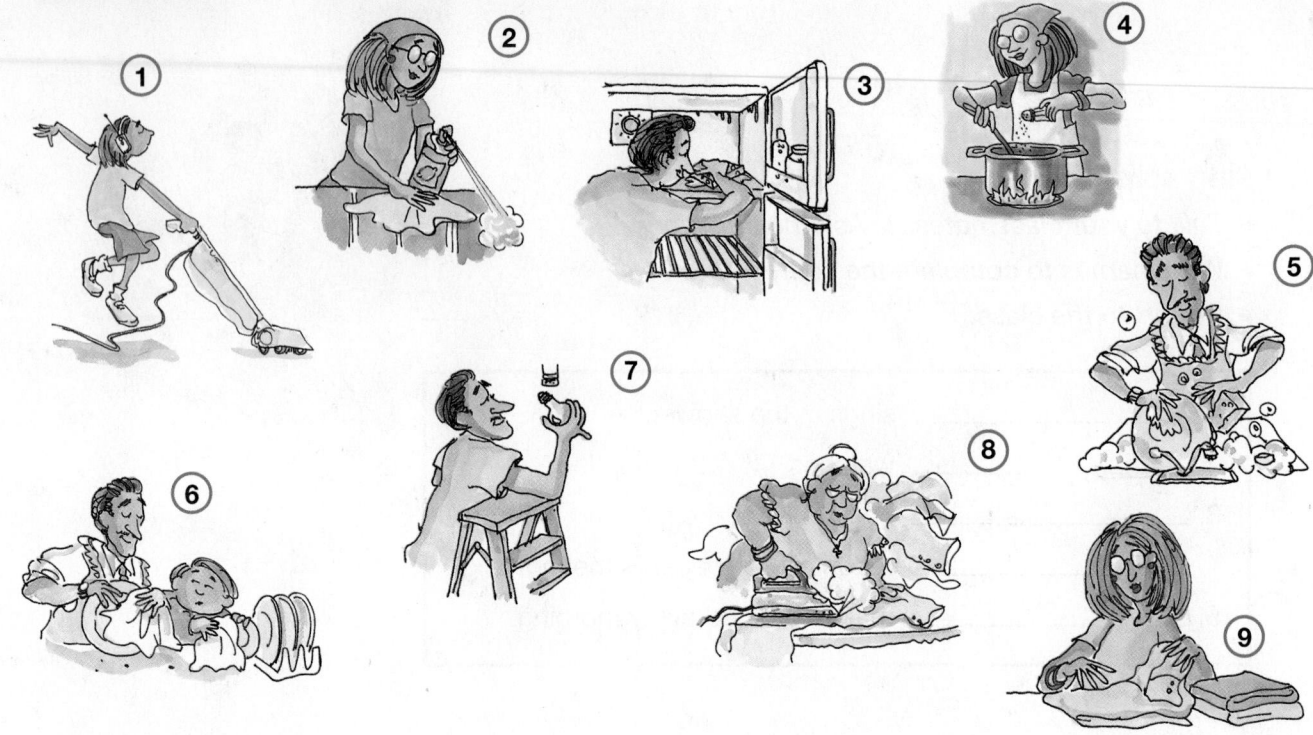

1. Doing housework

🎧 ▶ *Match the numbers and the words.** ▶ *Then listen and repeat.* ▶ *Add words.*

_____ a. change a light bulb	_____ e. dust	_____ i. wash the dishes
_____ b. clean the refrigerator	_____ f. fold the laundry	j. _____
_____ c. cook	_____ g. iron the clothes	k. _____
_____ d. dry the dishes	_____ h. vacuum	l. _____

2. Who does what?

▶ *Answer the questions with your class.*

1. What housework does the mother in the picture do? *[She cooks, dusts, and . . .]*

2. What housework does the father do?

3. What housework does the grandmother do?

4. What housework do the daughter and son do?

3. How about you?

▶ *Work with a partner.* ▶ *Ask and answer the questions.*

1. Who cooks at your house?

2. Who does the dishes?

3. Who dusts and vacuums?

   * Answers are on p. 179.

4. Do you do housework?

🎧 ▸ *Listen and repeat.* ▸ *Practice with a partner.*

JASMINE: Do you do housework, Greg?

GREG: Sure I do. I do the dishes. And sometimes I dust and vacuum. How about you, Jasmine? What housework do you do?

JASMINE: I cook every day, and I do the laundry every week.

5. A housework survey

▸ *Write answers to the questions.* ▸ *Work in a group.* ▸ *Ask and answer the questions.*

▸ *Report to the class.*

1. What housework do you do every day? _____

2. What housework do you do every week? _____

3. What housework do you never do? _____

6. Cross-cultural exchange

▸ *Work in a group.* ▸ *Ask and answer the questions.* ▸ *Report to the class.*

1. What housework do women usually do in your country?

2. What housework do men often do?

3. What housework do children usually do?

4. What housework does everyone do?

7. Conversation Chant: Lazy Susan

🎧 ▸ *Listen.* ▸ *Listen and repeat.* ▸ *Chant with your class.*

Louise does the shopping

And cooks the rice,

Washes the dishes

And catches the mice.

What about Susan?

What does she do?

She talks on the phone from ten to two.

From two to three she watches TV.

Then from three to four she watches

some more.

Use your English!

▸ *Write a list of all the housework you do in one week.* ▸ *Tell your conversation partner.*

▸ *Ask your conversation partner:* **What housework do you do every day? Every week? Never?**

Lesson 5 Everyday Life

1. Barbara's day

🎧 ▸ *Match the numbers and the words.** ▸ *Then listen and repeat.* ▸ *Add words.*

_____ a. do the dishes	_____ e. make dinner	i. _____
_____ b. feed the baby	_____ f. read to the children	j. _____
_____ c. go shopping	_____ g. study	
_____ d. go to class	_____ h. sweep the floor	

2. Before or after?

▸ *Fill in the clocks.* ▸ *Answer the questions with your class.*

1. What time does Barbara do each task?

2. Does Barbara do the dishes before or after she goes to class? *[She does the dishes after . . .]*

3. Does she read to the children before or after she studies?

4. Does she feed the baby before or after she goes to school?

3. How about you?

▸ *Work with a partner.* ▸ *Ask and answer the questions.*

1. What do you do before class?

2. What do you do after class?

3. What do you do every day?

   * Answers are on p. 179.

4. Yesterday, today, tomorrow

🎧 ▶ *Look at the calendar.* ▶ *Listen and repeat.* ▶ *Answer the questions with your class.*

1. **Today** means this day. What day is today?

2. **Tomorrow** means the day after today. What day is tomorrow?

3. What is **the day after tomorrow**?

4. **Yesterday** means the day before today. What day was yesterday?

5. What was **the day before yesterday**?

5. Days of the week

▶ *What do you do each day of the week?* ▶ *Write your activities on the calendar for morning, afternoon, and evening.* ▶ *Work with a partner.* ▶ *Tell one thing you do on each day of the week.*

	SUNDAY	MONDAY	TUESDAY	WEDNESDAY	THURSDAY	FRIDAY	SATURDAY
MORNING							
AFTERNOON							
EVENING							

Use your English!

▶ *Write a THINGS TO DO TODAY list for one day.* ▶ *Do the things on your list.*

Lesson 6 — Telephone Calls

make a call

KITTY: Hello. May I speak to Roger, please?
ROGER'S FATHER: Who's calling, please?
KITTY: It's Kitty.
ROGER'S FATHER: Just a minute, please. Roger, it's for you.

leave a message

ANSWERING MACHINE: Hi. We're not home right now. Please leave a message.
HUSBAND: Hi, honey. I'm in Chicago. I can't get a plane home today. I'm sorry. See you tomorrow!

REGINA: Hello?
CALLER: Is Salah there?
REGINA: Salah? I think you have the wrong number.
CALLER: Is this area code (716) 969-1818?
REGINA: No. It's 1819.
CALLER: Oh. Sorry.

wrong number

1. Telephone calls

🎧 ▸ *Match the numbers and the words.* * ▸ *Then listen and repeat.* ▸ *Add words.*

_____ a. answering machine	_____ d. hang up	_____ g. phone cord
_____ b. cell phone	_____ e. pay phone	_____ h. receiver
_____ c. cordless phone	_____ f. phone card	i. _____

2. What's happening?

▸ *Answer the questions with your class.*

1. What's happening in each picture? *[Kitty is calling Roger from a cell phone . . .]*

2. Who's using a cell phone? A cordless phone? A pay phone? A phone with a cord?

3. Who's leaving a message? What's the message?

4. What's Regina's telephone number? What's her area code?

3. How about you?

▸ *Work with a partner.* ▸ *Ask and answer the questions.*

1. Do you have a telephone? Do you like to talk on the phone?

2. Do you have a cell phone? A cordless phone? An answering machine?

3. Who do you talk to on the phone? What language do you use?

   * Answers are on p. 179.

4. Role play

▶ *Work with a partner.* ▶ *Write phone conversations to make a call, leave a message, and call a wrong number.* ▶ *Present one of your role plays to the class.*

5. Prepaid phone cards

🎧 ▶ *Listen and repeat.* ▶ *Work with a partner.*

▶ *Answer the questions.*

1. How many minutes of calling time are on this phone card?
2. What numbers do you enter first?
3. What numbers do you enter next?
4. What numbers do you enter last?
5. What do you enter for international calls?

WORLD *Prepaid Phone Card*

575 minutes

Instructions:
1. Enter 1 + 800-405-6937.
2. Enter Card Number: 3044-9633-0102
THEN—FOR CALLS INSIDE USA:
Enter 1 + Area Code + Number
FOR INTERNATIONAL CALLS
Enter 011 + Country Code + City Code + Number

6. Cross-cultural exchange

▶ *Work in a group.* ▶ *Ask and answer the questions.* ▶ *Report to the class.*

1. Are cell phones popular in your country? Do people use answering machines?
2. Do you ever make international calls? If yes, what country or countries do you call? What numbers do you have to dial?
3. Do people use pay phones in your country? Do they use prepaid phone cards? How much does a local call cost?

7. Find someone who . . .

▶ *Talk to your classmates.* ▶ *Ask the questions.* ▶ *Write names to complete the sentences.*

▶ *Report to the class.*

1. _____ has a cell phone.
2. _____ has a cordless phone.
3. _____ has an answering machine.
4. _____ talks on the phone every day.
5. _____ likes to use English on the phone.

Use your English!

▶ *Use your local telephone book.* ▶ *Find and write down phone numbers for your school and the phone company business office.*

_____   _____

LISTENING PRACTICE

1. What do you hear?

🎧 ▸ *Listen.* ▸ *Circle a or b.* *

1. a. When do you sweep?
   b. When do you sleep?
2. a. Is that your mother?
   b. Is that your brother?
3. a. This is my wife.
   b. This is my life.
4. a. I leave for work at 7:15.
   b. I leave for work at 7:50.
5. a. Is it 8:30 now?
   b. Is it 8:13 now?

6. a. She gets up at 6:14.
   b. She gets up at 6:40.
7. a. What does he do first?
   b. What does he do fifth?
8. a. Does he do housework?
   b. Does she do housework?
9. a. Is that area code 212?
   b. Is that area code 202?

2. Questions and answers

🎧 ▸ *Listen.* ▸ *Circle a or b.* *

1. a. Every day.
   b. No, he doesn't.
2. a. No, he doesn't.
   b. Yes, she does.
3. a. I have six.
   b. I have two brothers
      and one sister.
4. a. No, I don't.
   b. Yes, I am.
5. a. She sweeps.
   b. She's sweeping.

6. a. Yes, I study every Saturday.
   b. Yes, I do vacuum and dust every Sunday.
7. a. At 7:00 A.M.
   b. At 10:30.
8. a. She's 47.
   b. He's 38.
9. a. She goes to school.
   b. Yes, she does.
10. a. Yes, he is.
    b. Yes, he does.

3. How about you?

🎧 ▸ *Listen.* ▸ *Write your answers.* ▸ *Work in a group.* ▸ *Read your answers to the class.*

1. _____

2. _____

3. _____

4. _____

* Answers are on p. 179.

REVIEW

1. **Get to know your partner.**
   ► *Work with a partner.* ► *Ask and answer questions about your families.* ► *Take notes.*
   ► *Tell the class about your partner.*

2. **What time . . . ?**
   ► *Complete the two questions.* ► *Write a third question.* ► *Walk around your classroom.*
   ► *Ask three students your questions.* ► *Then answer their questions.*
   1. What time is _____ ?
   2. What time do _____ ?
   3. _____ ?

3. **Housework: Who am I?**
   ► *On a piece of paper, write one kind of housework and how often you do it (every day, every week, always, often, sometimes, never).* ► *Fold your paper.* ► *Make a pile.* ► *Open one.*
   ► *Read it to the class.* ► *Guess who it is.*

4. **What do you do?**
   ► *Work with a partner.* ► *Ask and answer the questions.*
   1. What do you do first in the morning? Second? Third? Last?
   2. What do you usually do each day of the week?

5. **Favorite day**
   ► *Work with a group.* ► *Ask and answer the questions.*
   1. What's your favorite day of the week?
   2. Why?

ASSESSMENT

PART 1: Questions

▶ *Write questions to ask a classmate.*

1. Family: _____

2. Time: _____

3. Morning routine: _____

4. Housework: _____

5. Telephone: _____

PART 2: Speaking

▶ *Work with a partner.* ▶ *Ask and answer your questions from Part 1.*

PART 3: Listening

🎧 ▶ *Listen.* ▶ *Circle a or b.* *

1. a. Yes, she is.
   b. Yes, she does.

2. a. He watches TV.
   b. They practice their English.

3. a. She's 18.
   b. She's fine, thanks.

4. a. It's 6:30. He's getting up.
   b. He gets up and takes a shower.

5. a. Every day.
   b. Yes, I do the dishes.

6. a. I go to work.
   b. I leave for class.

PART 4: Writing

▶ *Write conversations for these pictures.*

HARRY: *What a cute baby!*

GRANDFATHER: *Thanks. She's my* _____

HARRY: *What's her name? How old is she?*

GRANDFATHER: _____

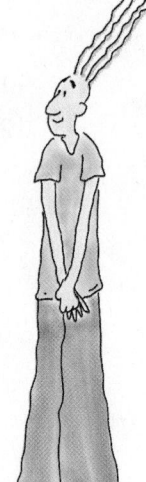

GREG: _____

JASMINE: _____

GREG: _____

JASMINE: _____

* Answers are on p. 179.

UNIT 3
YOUR HOME

PREVIEW

Preview Questions

▶ *Read the questions. What can you answer?*

1. What do you see in the first picture? What are the people doing?
2. What do you see in the second picture?
3. What things do you do at home?
4. What do you have to do at home today?
5. What do you want to do tonight?

Conversation Tip

▶ *Read the Conversation Tip.* ▶ *Practice with a partner.*

Ask **How do you say this in English?** *and* **How do you spell that?**
to learn new words.

A: **How do you say this in English?**
B: It's an oven.
A: An oven? **How do you spell that?**
B: O-v-e-n.

Conversation Chant: Kathy's Dog Moved to Paris 🎵

🎧 ▶ *Listen.* ▶ *Listen and repeat.* ▶ *Chant with your class.*

Kathy lives in a condo.

    Her apartment's on the 14th floor.

She's got a balcony with a wonderful view,

    But they don't allow dogs anymore.

Kathy's dog moved to Paris.

    He made his home on a bench.

He loves the dogs in Paris,

    And he's learning to bark in French!

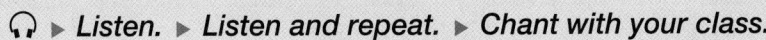

Lesson 1   Your Home

1. Homes

🎧 ▶ *Match the numbers and the words.** ▶ *Then listen and repeat.* ▶ *Add words.*

_____ a. apartment building	_____ e. house	_____ i. three floors
_____ b. balcony	_____ f. mobile home	_____ j. yard
_____ c. condominium	_____ g. roof	_____ k. fence
_____ d. garage	_____ h. stairs	l. _____

2. Different homes

▶ *Answer the questions with your class.*

1. What do all these homes have?

2. What's different about each?

3. Your home

▶ *Work with a partner.* ▶ *Ask and answer the questions.* ▶ *Tell the class about your partner's home.*

1. What kind of home do you live in? How many floors does it have?

2. Does it have a garage? A yard? A basement? A fence?

3. What else does your home have?

* Answers are on p. 179.

4. Lei's new phone number and address

🎧 ▶ *Listen and repeat.* ▶ *Practice with a partner.*

LEI: Hi, Mom. I'm calling from my new apartment. I love it!

MOTHER: That's wonderful, Lei! What's your new phone number?

LEI: It's area code (718) 555-6783.

MOTHER: And your address?

LEI: 219 East 57th Street, Apartment 16J, Bronx, New York. The ZIP code is 10471.

MOTHER: 10471. OK. Well, I'm glad you're happy, Lei. We miss you, honey.

LEI: I miss you all, too, Mom, and I miss Hawaii.

5. How about you?

▶ *Work with a partner.* ▶ *Ask and answer the questions.*

1. Do you have a phone? If yes, what's your phone number?

2. What street do you live on? Do you have an apartment number? If yes, what is it?

3. What city and state do you live in? What's your zip code?

4. Do you miss your friends or family? Who do you miss? Where are they?

6. Conversation Chant: A House Is Not a Home 🎵

🎧 ▶ *Listen.* ▶ *Listen and repeat.* ▶ *Chant with your class.*

Mary and her husband want to buy a house.

Their kids want a mobile home.

Mary wants to move to Portugal.

Her husband wants to live in Rome.

Mary doesn't like apartments.

She wants a place near the sea.

Her husband wants to have a big garage.

To park his SUV.

I hope the family find their dreams,

But a house is not a home.

I'm sure they'll be happy somewhere

In Portugal or Rome.

Use your English!

▶ *Ask your conversation partner:* **What's your address and phone number?**

Lesson 2 The Kitchen

What's in the kitchen?

_____ a. cabinet

_____ b. coffee maker

_____ c. dishwasher

_____ d. dryer

_____ e. electric mixer

_____ f. pan

_____ g. refrigerator

_____ h. sink

_____ i. stove

_____ j. toaster

_____ k. washing machine

l. _____

m. _____

What are the people doing?

_____ n. doing laundry

_____ o. making a sandwich

p. _____

q. _____

1. The kitchen

🎧 ▶ *Match the numbers and the words.** ▶ *Then listen and repeat.* ▶ *Add words.*

2. In the kitchen

▶ *Answer the questions with your class.*

1. What things are in this kitchen?

2. What are the people doing in the picture?

3. What is the dog doing?

3. How about you?

▶ *Work with a partner.* ▶ *Ask and answer the questions.*

1. What's in your kitchen?

2. What do you do in your kitchen?

* Answers are on p. 179.

4. The same or different?

▶ *Work in a group.* ▶ *Look at the kitchen on page 36. Look at the kitchen on this page. What's the same? What's different?*

▶ *Make lists.* ▶ *Share your lists with the class.*

WHAT'S THE SAME?

Example: *There are cabinets in both kitchens.*

1. _____
2. _____
3. _____
4. _____
5. _____
6. _____

WHAT'S DIFFERENT?

Example: *There's no washing machine in this kitchen.*

1. _____
2. _____
3. _____
4. _____
5. _____
6. _____

5. Find someone who . . .

▶ *Talk to your classmates.* ▶ *Ask the questions.* ▶ *Write the names to complete the sentences.*

▶ *Report to the class.*

1. _____ does laundry in the kitchen.
2. _____ uses an electric mixer.
3. _____ doesn't have a toaster.
4. _____ loves to make sandwiches.
5. _____ has a dishwasher.
6. _____ eats in the kitchen.

Use your English!

▶ *Ask your conversation partner:* **What do you have in your kitchen? What do you do in your kitchen?** ▶ *Tell your conversation partner about your kitchen.* ▶ *Make English labels for things in your kitchen.* ▶ *Practice the new vocabulary.*

Lesson 3 The Dining Area and Living Room

What's in the dining room?

_____ a. bowl

_____ b. fork

_____ c. glass

_____ d. knife

_____ e. napkin

_____ f. pitcher

_____ g. plate

_____ h. spoon

_____ i. tablecloth

j. _____

k. _____

What are the people doing?

_____ l. bringing the food

_____ m. pouring the milk

_____ n. setting the table

o. _____

p. _____

1. The dining room

🎧 ▸ *Match the numbers and the words.* * ▸ *Listen and repeat.* ▸ *Add words.*

2. What are they doing?

▸ *Answer the questions with your class.*

1. What is the sister doing? *[She's . . .]*

2. What is she putting on the table?

3. What are the brothers doing? *[One brother is . . .   The other brother is . . .]*

4. What is the mother doing?

3. How about you?

▸ *Work with a partner.* ▸ *Ask and answer the questions.*

1. Is there a dining room or a dining area in your home? What's in it?

2. Where do you eat dinner at home?

3. Who sets the table at your home? What does he or she put on the table at dinnertime?

* Answers are on p. 179.

4. The Living Room

🎧 ▸ *Match the numbers and the words.* ▸ *Then listen and repeat.* ▸ *Add words.*

What's in the living room?

_____ a. CD player

_____ b. DVD video player

_____ c. entertainment center

_____ d. headset

_____ e. lamp

_____ f. rug

_____ g. sofa

_____ h. table

i. _____

j. _____

What are the people doing?

_____ k. playing a video game

_____ l. using a laptop computer

m. _____

n. _____

5. What are they saying?

🎧 ▸ *Listen and repeat.* ▸ *Practice in a group of four.*

DAN: Do you want to play a video game with me, Ben?

BEN: Not now. I'm doing my homework.

DAN: How about you, Sally?

SALLY: No, thanks. I'm drawing a picture now.

DAN: How about you, Dad?

DAD: Sorry, son. I'm e-mailing my conversation partner for English class now.

6. In the living room

▸ *Answer the questions with your class.*

1. What's in this living room?   2. What's this family doing there?

7. How about you?

▸ *Work with a partner.* ▸ *Ask and answer the questions.*

1. Does your home have a living room? What's in it?

2. What do you do there?

Use your English!

▸ *Ask your conversation partner:* **What's in your living room? What do you do there?**

Lesson 4 Neat and Messy Bedrooms

a messy bedroom | a neat bedroom

1. Two bedrooms

🎧 ▸ *Match the numbers and the words.* ▸ *Then listen and repeat.* ▸ *Add words.*

_____ a. bedspread   _____ f. dresser   _____ k. slippers

_____ b. blanket   _____ g. hangers   l. _____

_____ c. mirror   _____ h. pajamas   m. _____

_____ d. closet   _____ i. pillow

_____ e. dirty dishes   _____ j. sheet

2. A neat and a messy bedroom

▸ *Answer the questions with your class.*

1. What is the same in both bedrooms? *[Both bedrooms have . . .]*

2. What is messy in the messy bedroom and neat in the neat bedroom?

3. What are they saying?

🎧 ▸ *Listen and repeat.* ▸ *Practice in a group of three.*

MRS. BROWN: Hello?

NICOLE: Hi, Mrs. Brown. It's Nicole. Is Briana there?

MRS. BROWN: Hello, Nicole. Yes, she is. Just a minute, please.

BRIANA: Hi, Nicole. How are you doing?

NICOLE: Great, thanks. Listen, do you want to go to a movie?

BRIANA: Yes, but I can't. I have to clean my room. It's really messy.

NICOLE: Too bad! OK, I'll talk to you soon. Bye!

BRIANA: Bye.

* Answers are on p. 179.

4. **Who's who?**

▶ *Answer the questions with your class.*

1. Which girl is Nicole? Which is Briana?

2. What are the girls wearing? What are they doing?

3. What does Briana want to do? What does she have to do? Why?

5. **Role play**

▶ *Work in a group of three.* ▶ *Complete the phone conversation.* ▶ *Present your role play to the class.*

A: Hello?

B: Hi, _____. It's _____. Is _____ there?

A: _____.

C: Hi, _____. How are you doing?

B: _____. Do you want to _____?

C: Yes, but I can't. I have to _____.

B: _____.

C: _____.

6. **How about you?**

▶ *Work with a partner.* ▶ *Ask and answer the questions.*

1. What's in your bedroom?

2. Is your bedroom usually neat or messy?

3. How often do you clean your bedroom?

7. **Neat or messy?**

▶ *Ask six classmates:* **Is your bedroom neat or messy?** ▶ *Check (✓) NEAT or MESSY.*

▶ *Report to the class.*

NAME	NEAT	MESSY
1. _____	☐	☐
2. _____	☐	☐
3. _____	☐	☐
4. _____	☐	☐
5. _____	☐	☐
6. _____	☐	☐

Use your English!

▶ *Ask your conversation partner* **What's your bedroom like? Is it usually neat or messy?** ▶ *Make English labels for things in your bedroom.* ▶ *Practice the new vocabulary.*

Lesson 5   The Bathroom

1. The bathroom

🎧 ▸ *Match the numbers and the words.* * ▸ *Then listen and repeat.* ▸ *Add words.*

_____ a. bathtub		_____ f. shampoo		_____ k. toothbrush
_____ b. bubble bath		_____ g. shaving cream		_____ l. toothpaste
_____ c. electric razor		_____ h. soap		_____ m. towel
_____ d. lipstick		_____ i. toilet		n. _____
_____ e. razor		_____ j. toilet paper		o. _____

2. What are they doing?

▸ *Work with a partner. Answer the questions.*

1. Who's taking a bath?
2. Who's putting on lipstick?
3. Who's brushing her teeth?

3. Your bathroom

▸ *Work with a partner. Ask and answer the questions.*

1. What's in your bathroom at home?
2. What color is your toothbrush? Your towel? Your bathroom sink?

* Answers are on p. 180.

4. A brand survey

▸ *Work in a group of three.* ▸ *Ask and answer about toothpaste, shampoo, and soap.*

▸ *Complete the chart.* ▸ *Tell the class about your partners.*

A: What brand of toothpaste do you use?

B: I use Bright toothpaste. How about you?

NAME	TOOTHPASTE	SOAP	SHAMPOO
1.			
2.			
3.			

5. Find someone who . . .

▸ *Talk to your classmates.* ▸ *Ask the questions.* ▸ *Write names to complete the sentences.*

▸ *Report to the class.*

NAME
1. _____ likes to take baths.
2. _____ usually takes showers.
3. _____ sometimes uses bubble bath.

6. Conversation Chant: Where's My Toothbrush?

🎧 ▸ *Listen.* ▸ *Listen and repeat.* ▸ *Chant with your class.*

Where's my toothbrush?

   It's next to the toothpaste.

Where's the toothpaste?

   It's next to your toothbrush.

Where's my shampoo?

   I don't know,

   But I think I saw it an hour ago.

Where's the bubble bath?

   It's on the floor.

Where are the towels?

   Behind the door.

Where's my lipstick?

   I don't know.

   But I'm sure I saw it an hour ago.

Use your English!

▸ *Ask your conversation partner:* **What kind of toothpaste do you use? What's your favorite brand of shampoo? What brand of soap do you like?** ▸ *Make English labels for the things in your bathroom.* ▸ *Practice the new vocabulary.*

Lesson 6 Problems at Home

mice and cockroaches

clogged toilet

no heat

1. Problems

🎧 ▶ *Match the numbers and the words.** ▶ *Then listen and repeat.* ▶ *Add words.*

_____ a. cockroach	_____ e. mouse/mice	_____ i. radiator
_____ b. clogged drain	_____ f. mousetrap	j. _____
_____ c. drain opener	_____ g. pesticide	k. _____
_____ d. exterminator	_____ h. plunger	l. _____

2. What are the problems?

▶ *Work with a partner.* ▶ *Match the problems and the sentences.* ▶ *Write the letters of two sentences next to each problem.**

1. Mice and Cockroaches: _____ _____

2. Clogged Toilet: _____ _____

3. No Heat: _____ _____

a. "The plunger and drain opener aren't working."
b. "My children and I are very cold."
c. "I have mice and cockroaches in my kitchen!"
d. "Our radiator isn't working."
e. "Please exterminate them for me!"
f. "The toilet's completely clogged!"

3. What's wrong?

▶ *Answer the questions with your class.*
1. What's the mice and cockroaches problem?
2. What's wrong with the toilet?
3. What's the heat problem?

* Answers are on p. 180.

4. Calling for help

🎧 ► *Listen.* ► *Listen and repeat.* ► *Practice with a partner.*

EXTERMINATOR: Ace Exterminators. May I help you?

CALLER: Hello. My name is Ann Rose, and I have a problem.

EXTERMINATOR: What's the problem, Ms. Rose?

CALLER: I have mice and cockroaches in my house! Can you help?

EXTERMINATOR: Yes, I can. I can come at 10:30 today. What's your address?

CALLER: 14 Holly Road. Thank you so much!

5. Who can they call?

► *Work in a group.* ► *Read the ads.* ► *Write a phone conversation for the toilet problem and the heat problem.* ► *Read your conversation to the class.*

6. Problems at home

► *Work in a group.* ► *Talk about problems you can have at home.* ► *Write your group list on the board.* ► *Compare lists with other groups.*

Example: *You can have problems with the dishwasher.*

Use your English!

► *Ask your conversation partner:* **What problems do you have at home?** ► *Tell your conversation partner about your problems at home.* ► *Use the Internet or your local telephone book.* ► *Find and write down the addresses and phone numbers for two plumbers and two exterminators.* ► *Report the information to the class.*

LISTENING PRACTICE

1. What do you hear?

🎧 ▸ *Listen.* ▸ *Circle a or b.**

1. a. Please don't park the car in the garage.
   b. Please don't park the car in the yard.
2. a. Her apartment number is 7J.
   b. Her apartment number is 7G.
3. a. Our address is 125 Main Street.
   b. Our address is 25 Main Street.
4. a. The ZIP code is 85469.
   b. The ZIP code is 85461.

5. a. The new apartment building has 33 stories.
   b. The new apartment building has 13 stories.
6. a. Please sit at the table.
   b. Please set the table.
7. a. What do you have to do today?
   b. What do you want to do today?
8. a. The kids' bathroom is really messy.
   b. The kids' bedroom is really messy.

2. Questions and answers

🎧 ▸ *Listen.* ▸ *Circle a or b.**

1. a. Yes, it's neat.
   b. No, it's not.
2. a. They're dirty.
   b. No, they're not.
3. a. She has to write a few e-mails.
   b. She doesn't want to go.
4. a. The toaster doesn't work.
   b. No, there isn't.
5. a. No, I don't. It's Sunday!
   b. Yes, but I can't. I have to do homework.

6. a. The washing machine and dryer are in the basement.
   b. Every weekend—usually on Saturday.
7. a. In New York City.
   b. 45 Third Avenue, Apartment 2H.
8. a. It's in my closet.
   b. They're in my dresser.
9. a. Thanks. It's from Mexico.
   b. Thank you. They're new.
10. a. Because we have cockroaches.
    b. Because I think we have mice.

3. About you

🎧 ▸ *Listen.* ▸ *Write your answers.* ▸ *Work in a group.* ▸ *Read your answers to the class.*

1. _____
2. _____
3. _____
4. _____

* Answers are on p. 180.

REVIEW

1. Make a list!

▸ *Work in a group.* ▸ *Look at the picture, and list words for each room.* ▸ *Share your lists with the class.*

2. How do you say this?

▸ *Choose an article in your classroom.* ▸ *Ask:* **How do you say this in English?** *Then ask:* **How do you spell that?** ▸ *Write the word on a piece of paper.* ▸ *Tape it to the article.*

3. How about you?

▸ *Walk around and talk to your classmates.* ▸ *Ask and answer these questions.*

1. What's your address?
2. Your e-mail address?
3. What do you do at home every night?
4. Is your home neat or messy?

4. What am I doing?

▸ *Work in a group.* ▸ *Act out an activity that you do in a room at home.* ▸ *Have the group guess the activity and the room.*

Example:

A: What am I doing? What room am I in?
B: You're getting dressed. You're in the bedroom.

ASSESSMENT

PART 1: Questions

▶ *Write questions to ask a classmate.*

1. Address: _____

2. Kitchen: _____

3. Living room or dining area: _____

4. Bedroom: _____

5. Bathroom: _____

PART 2: Speaking

▶ *Work with a partner.* ▶ *Ask and answer your questions from Part 1.*

PART 3: Listening

🎧 ▶ *Listen.* ▶ *Circle a or b.* *

1. a. It's a refrigerator.
   b. I call my sister almost every day.

2. a. It has two stories.
   b. No, in an apartment.

3. a. It's in the cabinet.
   b. They're under the entertainment center.

4. a. The toilet is clogged.
   b. We have cockroaches in the bathroom.

5. a. I know. I have to clean it.
   b. No, it isn't. It's very messy.

6. a. In the living room.
   b. In the evening.

PART 4: Writing

▶ *Write a conversation for this picture.*

EXTERMINATOR: _____

MAN: _____

EXTERMINATOR: _____

MAN: _____

   * Answers are on p. 180.

UNIT 4
FOOD

PREVIEW

Preview Questions

▶ *Read the questions. What can you answer?*

1. Where are the people in the picture?
2. What meal are they eating—breakfast, lunch, or dinner?
3. What foods are they eating?
4. What are they saying to each other?

Conversation Tip

▶ *Read the Conversation Tip.* ▶ *Practice with a partner.*

Say **please** *and* **thank you** *or* **thanks** *to be polite.*

A: Would like you more coffee?
B: Yes, **please**.

A: Would you like more chicken?
B: No, **thank you.**

A: Two pounds of oranges, **please**.
B: OK. Anything else?
A: No, **thanks**.

A: **Please** pass the bread.
B: Here you are.
A: **Thanks**.

Conversation Chant: It's Time to Eat!

🎧 ▶ *Listen.* ▶ *Listen and repeat.* ▶ *Chant with your class.*

He's hungry.

So is she.

She's starving!

So are we.

We're very hungry.

So is Pete.

What time is it?

It's time to eat!

Lesson 1 Vegetables

1. Vegetables

🎧 ▶ *Match the numbers and the words.** ▶ Then listen and repeat.* ▶ *Add words.*

_____ a. broccoli	_____ f. green beans	_____ k. potatoes
_____ b. carrots	_____ g. lettuce	_____ l. tomatoes
_____ c. celery	_____ h. mushrooms	m. _____
_____ d. corn	_____ i. onions	n. _____
_____ e. cucumbers	_____ j. peppers	o. _____

2. How about you?

▶ *Work with a partner.* ▶ *Ask and answer the questions.*

1. What vegetables do you like? _____

2. What vegetables don't you like? _____

3. What vegetables do you usually eat? _____

4. What vegetables do people in your country eat? _____

    * Answers are on p. 180.

3. Let's make a salad.

🎧 ▶ *Listen and repeat.* ▶ *Practice with a partner.*

A: Let's make a big salad!

B: Great idea. What do we need?

A: Well, we have lettuce and tomatoes, but we need cucumbers, carrots, and onions.

B: OK. Let's get started.

4. What do you need?

▶ *Work with a partner.* ▶ *Make a list of the vegetables you need for each dish.* ▶ *Report to the class.*

POTATO SALAD

_____
_____
_____
_____

VEGETABLE SOUP

_____
_____
_____
_____

5. Conversation Chant: He Likes Cucumbers. 🎵

🎧 ▶ *Listen.* ▶ *Listen and repeat.* ▶ *Chant with your class.*

He likes cucumbers.

So does she.

She likes tomatoes.

So do we.

We like green beans.

So do they.

They eat green beans every day.

I like corn and celery, too.

I like mushrooms. Do you?

I love mushrooms and carrots, too.

I love vegetables.

I do too!

Use your English!

▶ *With your conversation partner, visit a vegetable stand or a supermarket.*

▶ *List all the vegetables you see.* ▶ *Tell your class.*

Lesson 2 Fruit

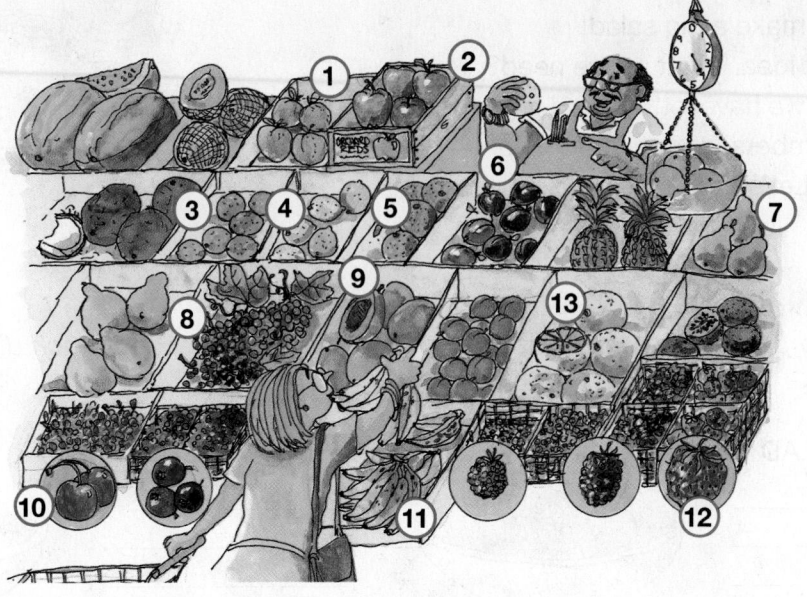

1. Fruit market

🎧 ▸ *Match the numbers and the words.* ▸ *Then listen and repeat.* ▸ *Add words.*

_____ a. apples		_____ f. lemons		_____ k. pears		
_____ b. bananas		_____ g. limes		_____ l. plums		
_____ c. cherries		_____ h. mangos		_____ m. strawberries		
_____ d. grapefruit		_____ i. oranges		n. _____		
_____ e. grapes		_____ j. peaches		o. _____		

2. What are they saying?

🎧 ▸ *Listen and repeat.* ▸ *Practice with a partner.*

GROCER: May I help you?

CUSTOMER: Yes. I'd like four pounds of oranges.

GROCER: OK.

CUSTOMER: I'd also like five bananas, please.

GROCER: All right. Anything else? How about some grapefruit?

CUSTOMER: No, thanks. I'm all set.

3. Role play

▸ *Work with a partner.* ▸ *Write a conversation at the fruit market.* ▸ *Present your role play to the class.*

4. What's your favorite fruit?

▸ *Walk around the classroom.* ▸ *Ask four students* **What's your favorite fruit?**

▸ *Report to the class.*

   * Answers are on p. 180.

5. Let's make a fruit salad!

▶ *Work in a group.* ▶ *Plan and then make a fruit salad.* ▶ *Get ready:*

What fruit can each student bring?

NAME	FRUIT

Who can bring a serving bowl?

_____

Who can bring a knife?

_____

Who can bring a serving spoon?

_____

Who can bring forks?

_____

Who can bring plates?

_____

▶ *Prepare your group's fruit salad.*

▶ *Vote on the best one.*

▶ *Compare the fruit salads.*

▶ *Enjoy the snack.*

Use your English!

▶ *Ask your conversation partner:* **What fruits do you like?** ▶ *Visit a fruit market or a supermarket.* ▶ *List all the fruits.* ▶ *Read your list to your class.*

Lesson 3 The Supermarket

_____ a. beef

_____ b. butter

_____ c. canned beans

_____ d. chicken

_____ e. cookies

_____ f. fish

_____ g. frozen dinners

_____ h. grocery cart

_____ i. ice cream

_____ j. milk

_____ k. pork

_____ l. _____

_____ m. _____

_____ n. _____

1. At the supermarket

🎧 ▶ *Match the numbers and the words.** ▶ Then listen and repeat. ▶ Add words.*

2. Where can I find the milk?

🎧 ▶ *Listen and repeat.* ▶ *Practice with a partner.*

CUSTOMER: Excuse me. Where can I find the milk?

CLERK: In the dairy section.

CUSTOMER: Thanks.

3. Excuse me.

▶ *Work with a partner.* ▶ *Write a conversation at the supermarket.* ▶ *Present your role play to the class.*

* Answers are on p. 180.

4. Specials of the week

▸ *Work with a partner.* ▸ *Write the prices and quantities from the ads.* ▸ *Compare the two markets.* ▸ *Report to the class.*

† oz = ounce pt = pint
  lb = pound qt = quart
  16 oz = 1 lb gal= gallon

1 gal = 4 qt = 8 pt

FOOD	JOHNNIE'S GROCERY		SUPER MART	
	Price	Quantity	Price	Quantity
chicken				
orange juice				
bread				
ice cream				

5. What supermarkets do you recommend?

▸ *Work in a group.* ▸ *Ask and answer the questions.*

1. What supermarkets are close to your home?
2. Where do you usually buy food?
3. What supermarkets do you recommend?

Use your English!

▸ *With your conversation partner, go to a supermarket.* ▸ *Choose three items.* ▸ *Note their prices.* ▸ *Report to the class.*

Lesson 4   Breakfast

1. Breakfast

🎧 ▶ *Match the numbers and the words.** ▶ *Then listen and repeat.* ▶ *Add words.*

_____ a. bacon and eggs	_____ f. hot cereal	_____ k. sugar
_____ b. cold cereal	_____ g. hot cocoa	_____ l. toast
_____ c. coffee	_____ h. jelly	m. _____
_____ d. Danish	_____ i. muffin	n. _____
_____ e. French toast	_____ j. pancakes	o. _____

2. What are they eating for breakfast?

▶ *Answer the questions with your class.*

1. What is this family eating for breakfast?

2. What foods are on the table?

3. Do you eat any of these foods for breakfast?

4. How are American breakfasts different from breakfasts in your country?

3. What are they saying?

🎧 ▸ *Listen and repeat.* ▸ *Practice with a partner.*

SISTER: Please pass the muffins.

BROTHER: Here you are.

SISTER: Thanks.

MOTHER: Would you like more orange juice, dear?

FATHER: Yes, please.

MOTHER: Would you like more coffee?

FATHER: No, thanks. I'm all set.

4. Role play

▸ *Work in a group.* ▸ *Write a conversation about breakfast.* ▸ *Present your role play to the class.*

5. How about you?

▸ *Work with a partner.* ▸ *Ask and answer the questions.*

1. What's your favorite breakfast?
2. What does your family eat for breakfast?
3. Do you ever have breakfast at a restaurant? What do you eat? What do you drink?
4. Do you ever skip breakfast?

6. Your classmates' breakfast

▸ *Ask five classmates:* **What do you eat for breakfast?** ▸ *Write their names and answers.*

▸ *Tell the class.*

NAME	BREAKFAST

Use your English!

▸ *With your conversation partner, go to a restaurant that serves breakfast.* ▸ *Have breakfast together.* ▸ *Speak English.*

Lesson 5 Lunch

1. Lunch

🎧 ▶ *Match the numbers and the words.** ▶ *Then listen and repeat.* ▶ *Add words.*

_____ a. cash register		_____ e. french fries		_____ i. soft drink	
_____ b. cheeseburger		_____ f. hamburgers		_____ j. straws	
_____ c. chicken nuggets		_____ g. in line		k. _____	
_____ d. drive-thru		_____ h. salad bar		l. _____	

2. What's happening?

▶ *Answer the questions with your class.*

1. What can you buy for lunch at this fast-food restaurant?
2. What is the woman buying for lunch?
3. How much does it cost?
4. What does her son want?
5. What do you think the people in line want?

3. How about you?

▶ *Work with a partner.* ▶ *Ask and answer the questions.*

1. Do you eat fast food? Where do you buy it?
2. What fast food do you like?
3. What do you usually eat for lunch?
4. Where do you usually eat lunch? What time?

* Answers are on p. 180.

4. What's the special today?

🎧 ▸ *Listen and repeat.* ▸ *Practice with a partner.*

a cafeteria

CUSTOMER: What's your special today?

SERVER: Today our lunch special is a roast beef
sandwich and a bowl of soup.

CUSTOMER: Hmm. What's the soup today?

SERVER: Mushroom soup.

CUSTOMER: I'd like the lunch special, please.

SERVER: Coming right up!

5. Role play

▸ *Work with a partner.* ▸ *Write a conversation in a cafeteria.* ▸ *Present your role play to the class.*

6. Cross-cultural exchange

▸ *Answer the questions with your class.*

1. Lunch is usually around noon in the U.S. What time is lunch in your country?

2. Lunch is usually a small meal in the U.S. Is it small or large in your country?

3. What foods do people eat for lunch in your country?

7. Find someone who...

▸ *Talk to your classmates.* ▸ *Ask the questions.* ▸ *Write names to complete the sentences.*

▸ *Report to the class.*

1. _____ likes fast food.
2. _____ never eats fast food.
3. _____ eats lunch at home.
4. _____ brings lunch from home.
5. _____ has lunch in a cafeteria.
6. _____ likes sandwiches.
7. _____ likes soup.

Use your English!

▸ *Ask your conversation partner:* **What's your favorite lunch? What fast foods do you like?**

Lesson 6   Dinner

1. Dinner

🎧 ▶ *Match the numbers and the words.* ▶ *Then listen and repeat.* ▶ *Add words.*

_____ a. chopsticks	_____ e. rice bowl	_____ i. teapot
_____ b. cushion	_____ f. roast beef	_____ j. wine glass
_____ c. dinner roll	_____ g. table leg	k. _____
_____ d. garden salad	_____ h. teacups	l. _____

2. What's different?

▶ *Answer the questions with your class.*

1. What are the two families eating?

2. What are they drinking?

3. What utensils are they using to eat with?

4. What are they sitting on?

5. What's different about the two tables?

* Answers are on p. 180.

3. How about you?

▶ *Work with a partner.* ▶ *Ask and answer the questions.*

1. In your home, do you eat dinner at a table? What do you sit on?
2. What utensils do you use to eat with?
3. Who eats dinner with you?
4. What do you like to eat and drink for dinner?
5. How often do you eat dinner at home? How often do you eat out?

4. Cross-cultural Exchange

▶ *Answer the questions with your class.*

1. What are some traditional dining customs in your country?
2. What are some traditional dinners in your country?
3. Are any dining customs in your country the same as these pictures?
4. Do you ever eat food from other countries in restaurants? What kinds of food?

5. Conversation Chant: Let's Eat In.

🎧 ▶ *Listen.* ▶ *Listen and repeat.* ▶ *Chant with your class.*

Let's eat in.

Let's eat out.

I feel like a steak.

I want trout.

There's a new French restaurant.

Come on, let's try it.

Not tonight. I'm on a diet.

Let's eat out.

Let's eat in.

No take-out, please. I want to stay thin.

There's a wonderful pizza place right

across the street.

Forget your diet! Come on, let's eat!

Use your English!

▶ *Ask your conversation partner:* **How often do you eat dinner at home? How often do you go out for dinner?** ▶ *Do a survey of your friends. Ask:* **What's your favorite food from another country?** ▶ *Tell the class.*

LISTENING PRACTICE

1. What do they need?

🎧 ▶ *Listen to the supermarket conversations.* ▶ *Circle the items they need.* *

1. oranges   mangos   bananas   grapes

    pears   strawberries   peaches   apples

2. carrots   green beans   corn   celery

    chicken   potatoes   onions   green peppers

2. At the supermarket

🎧 ▶ *Listen to the conversations.* ▶ *Complete the signs.* *

3. Meals

🎧 ▶ *Listen.* ▶ *Circle a, b, or c.* *

CONVERSATION 1

What meal are they eating?

a. Breakfast

b. Lunch

c. Dinner

CONVERSATION 2

What meal are they eating?

a. Breakfast

b. Lunch

c. Dinner

CONVERSATION 3

Where are they?

a. At home

b. In a cafeteria

c. In a fast-food restaurant

CONVERSATION 4

Where are they?

a. At home

b. In a cafeteria

c. In a fast-food restaurant

* Answers are on p. 180.

REVIEW

1. Who is it?

▶ *Write your answers on a piece of paper.* ▶ *Fold your paper.* ▶ *Make a pile.* ▶ *Open one.*

▶ *Read it to the class.* ▶ *Guess who it is.*

1. What's your favorite breakfast?

2. What's your favorite lunch?

3. What's your favorite dinner?

2. Find someone who . . .

▶ *Talk to your classmates.* ▶ *Ask the questions.* ▶ *Write names to complete the sentences.*

▶ *Report to the class.*

1. _____ eats dinner after 8:00 P.M.

2. _____ doesn't usually eat breakfast.

3. _____ likes to cook.

4. _____ never cooks.

5. _____ never eats sandwiches for lunch.

6. _____ usually eats breakfast at home.

3. Role Play

▶ *Work with a partner.* ▶ *Complete the conversations.* ▶ *Present one of your role plays to another pair of students.*

AT A FRUIT OR VEGETABLE STAND

A: May I help you?

B: _____

A: OK. Anything else?

B: _____

AT THE SUPERMARKET

A: Excuse me _____?

B: _____

A: Thanks.

AT THE TABLE

A: Please, _____

B: _____

A: Thanks.

ASSESSMENT

PART 1: Questions

▶ *Write questions to ask a classmate.*

1. Vegetables and fruit: _____

2. Breakfast: _____

3. Lunch: _____

4. Dinner: _____

PART 2: Speaking

▶ *Work with a partner.* ▶ *Ask and answer your questions from Part 1.*

PART 3: Listening

🎧 ▶ *Listen.* ▶ *Circle a or b.**

1. a. In the dairy section, over there.
   b. In the frozen foods in Aisle 4.

2. a. No, thanks. I'm all set.
   b. Here you are.

3. a. Half a sandwich and a bowl of soup.
   b. Coming right up!

4. a. In the produce section, over there.
   b. In the seafood section, over there.

5. a. Yes, please.
   b. OK. Let's go!

6. a. Great idea.
   b. Yes, I'd like four pounds of plums, please.

7. a. Orange juice, toast, and eggs.
   b. Hamburgers, french fries, and a soft drink.

8. a. Cookies are.
   b. Mangos are.

PART 4: Writing

▶ *Write a conversation for this picture.*

GROCER: May I help you?

CUSTOMER: _____

GROCER: _____

CUSTOMER: _____

GROCER: _____

CUSTOMER: _____

UNIT 5
YOUR COMMUNITY

PREVIEW

Preview Questions

▶ *Read the questions. What can you answer?*

1. What do you see in the picture?
2. What are the people doing?
3. What are they saying?

Conversation Tip

▶ *Read the Conversation Tip.* ▶ *Practice with a partner.*

Repeat information to be sure you understand.

A: How do I get to Central Bank?

B: Central Bank? Go straight. Go past Main Street. Central Bank is on the left.

A: **I go straight. I go past Main Street, and it's on the left?**

B: That's right.

A: Thank you.

Conversation Chant: Nice Neighborhood 🎵

🎧 ▶ *Listen.* ▶ *Listen and repeat.* ▶ *Chant with your class.*

Do you like your neighborhood?

    Yes, I do. The neighbors are nice,

    And they're quiet, too.

Do you have good restaurants?

    Yes, we do. We have lots of

    restaurants,

    And coffee shops, too.

How about movie theaters?

We have four,

    And at the mall, there are more.

Do you have a park?

    Yes, we do—a beautiful park and

    A fabulous zoo.

It sounds like a wonderful place to be.

Do you think you can find an

apartment for me?

Lesson 1 Neighborhood and Neighbors

1. The neighborhood

🎧 ▶ *Match the numbers and the words.** ▶ *Then listen and repeat.* ▶ *Add words.*

What's in the neighborhood?

_____ a. apartment building

_____ b. community garden

_____ c. mailbox

_____ d. parking space

_____ e. playground

_____ f. recycling

_____ g. sidewalk

_____ h. trash cans

i. _____

What are the people doing?

_____ j. buying ice cream

_____ k. playing in the street

_____ l. riding a bike

_____ m. visiting with each other

_____ n. walking the dog

o. _____

2. What's happening?

▶ *Answer the questions with your class.*

1. What places and things are in the neighborhood?

2. What's happening in this neighborhood? What are the people doing?

* Answers are on p. 180.

3. How do you like your neighborhood?

🎧 ▶ *Listen and repeat.* ▶ *Practice with a partner.*

1. A: How do you like your neighborhood?
   B: I like it a lot!
      It's nice. There's a community garden and a playground nearby.
   A: Is it safe?
   B: Children play in the streets. Neighbors walk their
      dogs and visit with one another.
   A: How wonderful!

2. A: How do you like your neighborhood?
   B: I don't like it at all.
   A: Why not?
   B: There are too many trash cans on the sidewalks, and
      there aren't enough parking spaces.
   A: That's too bad. Is it noisy?
   B: Yes, it's very noisy. There are too many children in the street and too
      many dogs.
   A: How horrible!

4. How about you?

▶ *Work with a partner.* ▶ *Ask and answer the questions.*

1. How do you like your neighborhood?
2. Do you like your neighbors? Are they friendly? Helpful? Angry? Noisy?
3. How can neighbors help one another? Do your neighbors help you? If yes, how?
4. What kinds of problems can people have with their neighbors?
5. What problems do you have with your neighbors?

Use your English!

▶ *Ask your conversation partner:* **Do you like your neighborhood? Why?**

Lesson 2   Around Town

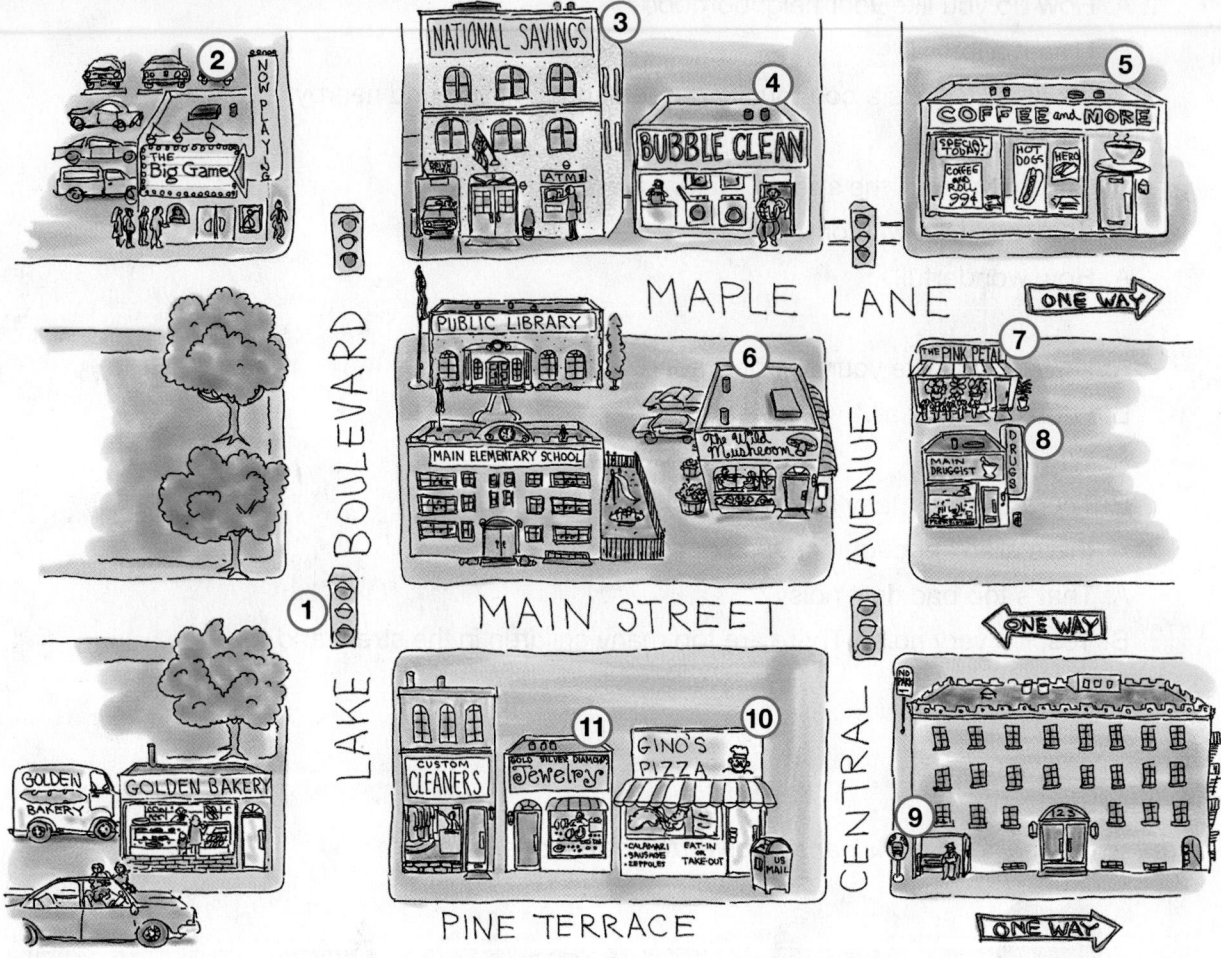

1. Community map

🎧 ▸ *Match the numbers and the words.** ▸ *Then listen and repeat.* ▸ *Add words.*

_____ a. bank	_____ f. grocery store	_____ k. traffic light
_____ b. bus stop	_____ g. jewelry store	l. _____
_____ c. coffee shop	_____ h. laundromat	m. _____
_____ d. drugstore	_____ i. movie theater	n. _____
_____ e. florist	_____ j. pizzeria	o. _____

2. What's in this community?

▸ *Work in a group.* ▸ *Answer the questions.* ▸ *Report to the class.*

1. What places and things are in the community in the picture? *[There's a . . . There are . . .]*
2. What is in your community?

* Answers are on p. 180.

3. Where is it?

🎧 ▶ *Listen and repeat.* ▶ *Practice with a partner.* ▶ *With your partner, add one more question and answer.*

1. Q: Where's the drugstore?
   A: It's **on** Central Avenue.

2. Q: Where's the grocery store?
   A: It's **across from** the drugstore.

3. Q: Where's the laundromat?
   A: It's **next to** the bank.

4. Q: Where's the movie theater?
   A: It's **on the corner of** Lake Boulevard **and** Maple Lane.

5. Q: Where's the jewelry store?
   A: It's **between** the cleaners **and** the pizzeria.

6. Q: Where's the _____ ?
   A: It's _____ .

4. What are they saying?

🎧 ▶ *Listen and repeat.* ▶ *Practice with a partner.*

A: Excuse me. How do I get to Gino's Pizzeria?

B: Gino's Pizzeria? Go straight; go past the cleaners and the jewelry store. Gino's Pizzeria is on the left.

A: Go straight; go past the cleaners and the jewelry store, and it's on the left?

B: That's right.

A: Thank you.

5. Role play

▶ *Work with a partner.* ▶ *Write a conversation to ask for and give directions.* ▶ *Present your role play to the class.*

Use your English!

- ▶ *With your conversation partner, choose a place in your community.*
- ▶ *Ask someone for directions to get there.*

Lesson 3 The Post Office

1. The post office

🎧 ▸ *Match the numbers and the words.** ▸ *Then listen and repeat.* ▸ *Add words.*

_____ a. book of stamps	_____ e. package	_____ i. stamp machine
_____ b. letter	_____ f. postal clerk	j. _____
_____ c. mail carrier	_____ g. postcard	k. _____
_____ d. mailbox	_____ h. stamp	l. _____

2. What can you do at the post office?

▸ *Answer the questions with your class.*

1. What can you mail at the post office?

2. What can you buy there?

   * Answers are on p. 180.

3. Post office conversations

🎧 ▶ *Listen and repeat.* ▶ *Practice with a partner.*

1. POSTAL CLERK: Can I help you?

CUSTOMER: Yes. I'd like to mail this package to Montreal.

POSTAL CLERK: How do you want to send it?

CUSTOMER: Priority mail. How long does it take to get there?

POSTAL CLERK: About two days.

2. POSTAL CLERK: Can I help you?

CUSTOMER: Yes. I'd like a stamp for this postcard.

POSTAL CLERK: Here you are. Anything else?

CUSTOMER: Yes. I'd also like a book of stamps.

4. Role play

▶ *Work with a partner.* ▶ *Write a conversation about the post office.* ▶ *Present your role play to the class.*

5. Conversation Chant: Lots of Mail

🎧 ▶ *Listen.* ▶ *Listen and repeat.* ▶ *Chant with the class.*

Letters, postcards, packages, too.

So much mail! I don't know what to do.

This mountain of letters never ends.

You need a bigger mailbox

Or fewer friends!

6. How often . . . ?

▶ *Work in a group.* ▶ *Ask and answer the questions.* ▶ *Count the answers and report to the class.*

HOW OFTEN DO YOU...	ONCE A WEEK	ONCE A MONTH	ONCE A YEAR	NEVER
1. go to the post office?				
2. write or receive letters?				
3. send or receive packages?				

Use your English!

▶ *Ask your conversation partner:* **Do you write letters? When do you go to the post office? What do you buy there?**

Lesson 4 The Bank

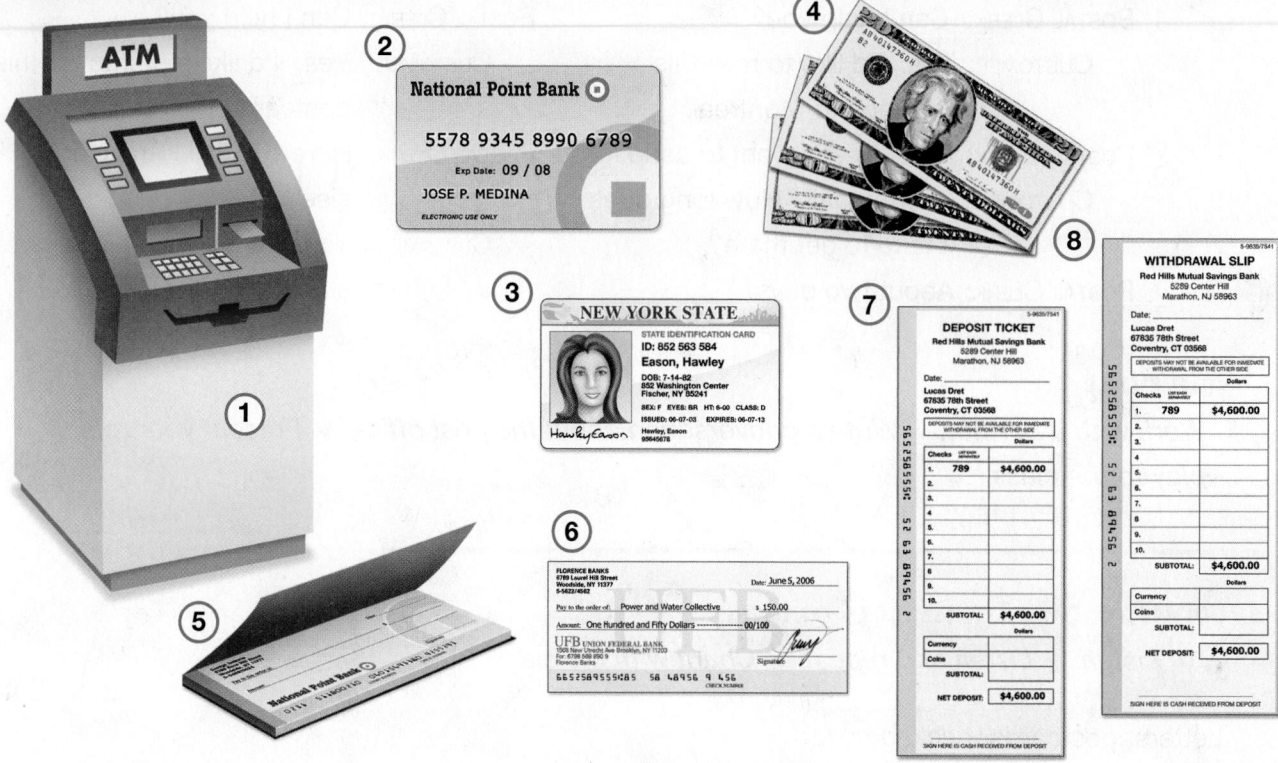

1. Banking items

🎧 ▶ *Match the numbers and the words.* ▶ *Then listen and repeat.*

_____ a. ATM   _____ d. checkbook   _____ g. identification

_____ b. cash   _____ e. debit card (ATM card)   _____ h. withdrawal slip

_____ c. check   _____ f. deposit slip

2. Banking

▶ *Answer the questions with your class.*

What do you need. . .

   a. to make a deposit to your savings account?

   b. to make a withdrawal from your savings account?

   c. to get cash from an ATM?

   d. to make a deposit to your checking account?

   e. to cash a check?

* Answers are on p. 180.

3. May I help you?

🎧 ▶ *Listen and repeat.* ▶ *Practice with a partner.* ▶ *Write another conversation at the bank.* ▶ *Present your role play to the class.*

TELLER: May I help you?

CUSTOMER: Yes, I'd like to make a deposit to my savings account. Here's my check, and deposit slip.

TELLER: May I see some identification?

CUSTOMER: Of course.

4. How about you?

▶ *Work with a partner.* ▶ *Ask and answer the questions.*

1. What bank do you use?

2. Do you like it? Why?

3. What do you do at the bank?

5. What do you do?

▶ *Work in a group.* ▶ *Look at the pictures and answer the questions.* ▶ *Report to the class.*

1. You cash a check for $50, and the teller gives you $60.
   What do you do?
   a. I take the money and say, "Thank you!"
   b. I say, "Excuse me. The check is for $50, not $60."
   c. I say, "_____"

2. You are a teller. A man says to you, "Give
   me all the money!" What do you do?
   a. I give him the money. After he leaves, I tell
      security.
   b. I press the security alarm while I give him the money.
   c. I shout, "Help! Police!"
   d. I _____.

Use your English!

▶ *With your conversation partner, find out:* **What banks are there in your community?**

▶ *Report to the class.*

Lesson 5 Help! Fire!

1. A fire

🎧 ▸ *Match the numbers and the words.** ▸ *Then listen and repeat.* ▸ *Add words.*

What's in the picture?		**What are the firefighters doing?**
_____ a. ambulance	_____ e. fire hydrant	_____ k. breaking down the door
_____ b. Emergency Medical	_____ f. fire truck	_____ l. putting out the fire
Technician (EMT)	_____ g. ladder	_____ m. saving someone
_____ c. fire escape	_____ h. oxygen	n. _____
_____ d. firefighter	_____ i. smoke	
	j. _____	

2. What's happening?

▸ *Answer the questions with your class.*

1. What's happening in the picture?

2. How many firefighters are there? What are they doing?

3. What are the EMTs doing?

4. Why is an ambulance there?

* Answers are on p. 180.

3. Reporting a fire

▶ *Work with a partner.* ▶ *Complete the conversation.* ▶ *Present your role play to the class.*

OPERATOR: 911. This call is being recorded. What's the emergency?

CALLER: _____

OPERATOR: Where are you calling from? What's the address?

CALLER: _____

OPERATOR: What's your name and phone number?

CALLER: _____

OPERATOR: Where's the fire?

CALLER: _____

Operator: What's happening now?

CALLER: _____

OPERATOR: Is anyone hurt?

CALLER: _____

OPERATOR: A fire truck and an ambulance are on the way.

4. How about you?

▶ *Answer the questions with your class.*

1. What should you do if there's a fire in your home?

2. Do you have any experience with fires? What happened?

---

5. Conversation Chant: Firefighters Climbing

🎧 ▶ *Listen.* ▶ *Listen and repeat.* ▶ *Chant with your class.*

Firefighters climbing, higher and higher,

Breaking down a door
To put out the fire.

A firefighter's strong and very brave.

The building's on fire,
And there are people to save.

Firefighters climbing higher and higher.

They know the lesson well:
"Where's there's smoke, there's fire."

Use your English!

▶ *Ask your conversation partner:* **Is there a fire station in your neighborhood? Where is it?**

Lesson 6 Help! Police!

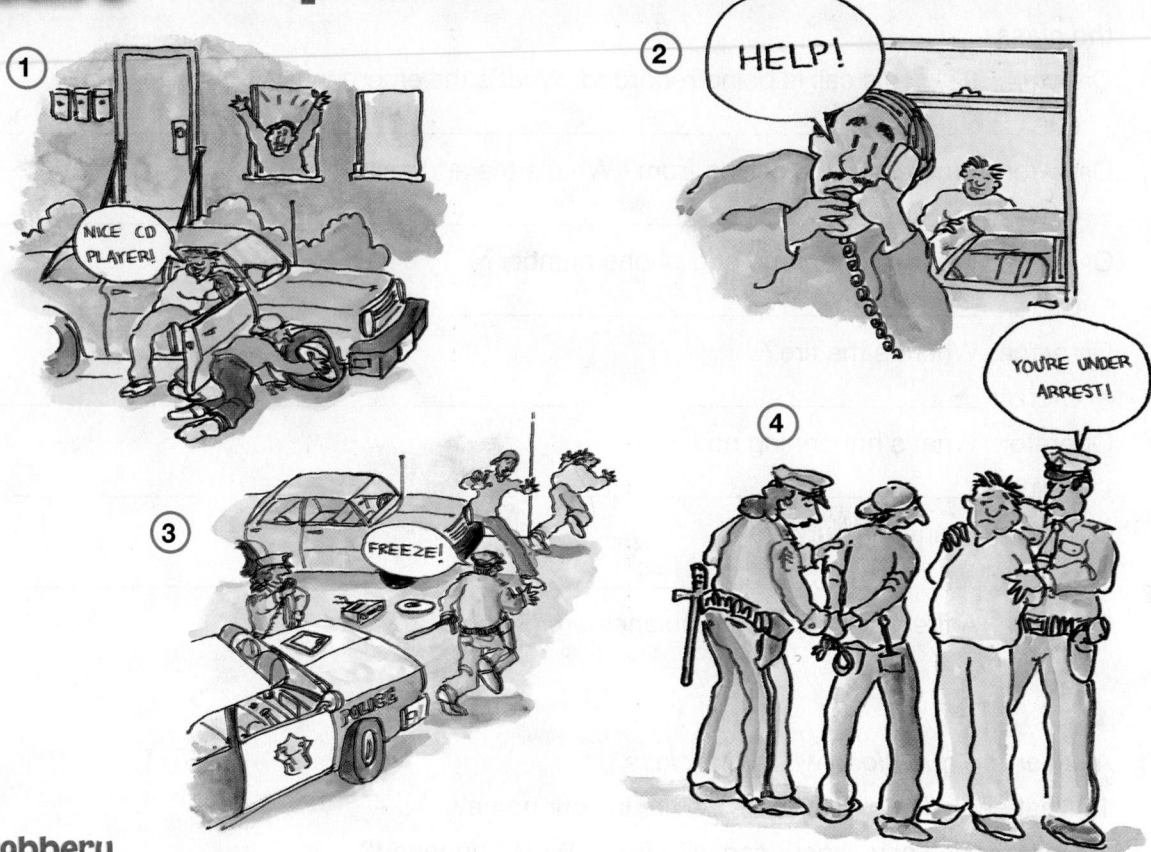

1. A robbery

🎧 ▶ *Match the numbers and sentences.** ▶ *Then listen and repeat.*

_____ a. Two young men break into Ernesto's car. They steal his CD player and his hubcaps.
Ernesto sees them.

_____ b. The police arrest the two robbers. They put handcuffs on them.

_____ c. The police arrive. They catch the two men.

_____ d. Ernesto calls 911. He reports the robbery.

2. What's the story?

▶ *Answer the questions with your class.*

1. Where is Ernesto?

2. What does he see through his window?

3. What does he do when he sees the robbers?

4. What do the robbers try to take?

5. Do the police arrive quickly after the call?

6. The police arrest the two robbers. Then what do they do?

3. Tell the story again.

▶ *Work with a partner.* ▶ *Look at the pictures and tell the story again.*

* Answers are on p. 181.

4. Role play

▶ *Work with a partner.* ▶ *Write a telephone conversation between Ernesto and the 911 operator.* ▶ *Present your role play to the class.*

5. What do you do?

▶ *Work with a partner.* ▶ *Read the questions. Check (✓) one or two answers.* ▶ *Add another answer.* ▶ *Report to the class.*

1. You lose your child on a busy city street. What do you do?

_____ a. I call 911.

_____ b. I call the non-emergency number for the police.

_____ c. I stay in the same place and wait for my child to find me.

_____ d. I tell people on the street, "I lost my child. Please help me!"

_____ e. I _____

2. You are lost. It's late at night, and you are alone. What do you do?

_____ a. I call 911.

_____ b. I ask a person in the street for directions.

_____ c. I continue to drive until I find my way.

_____ d. I drive to a store and ask for directions.

_____ e. I _____

6. When do you call 911?

▶ *Work with a group.* ▶ *Write three real emergencies.* ▶ *Read your emergencies to the class.*

1. _____

2. _____

3. _____

Use your English!

▶ *Find out: What is the telephone number for the police in your city or town?*

LISTENING PRACTICE

1. May I help you?

🎧 ▶ *Listen.* ▶ *Circle a or b.**

1. What is she mailing?
   a. A package
   b. A letter

2. How does she want to send it?
   a. First class
   b. Priority mail

3. How long does it take to get there?
   a. About three days
   b. About two weeks

2. 911

🎧 ▶ *Listen.* ▶ *Circle a or b.**

1. What's the emergency?
   a. A robbery
   b. A fire

2. Where is it?
   a. On Central Street
   b. On Main Street

3. What's happening?
   a. There's a lot of smoke.
   b. There are a lot of people.

3. Where is it?

🎧 ▶ *Listen to the conversations.*
▶ *Write the places on the map.**

1. Where is the movie theater?
2. Where is the drugstore?
3. Where is the school?

* Answers are on p. 181.

REVIEW

1. **Your neighborhood**
   ▶ *Draw a map of your neighborhood.* ▶ *Work with a partner.* ▶ *Show your map to your partner and talk about your neighborhood.*

2. **What's happening?**
   ▶ *Look out your classroom window or go outside.* ▶ *Write down what you see.*
   ▶ *Report to the class.*

3. **What's the place?**
   ▶ *Write your answers on a piece of paper.* ▶ *Fold your paper.* ▶ *Make a pile.* ▶ *Open one.*
   ▶ *Read it to the class.* ▶ *Guess what it is.*
   Think of a place in your school's neighborhood.
   1. Where is it?
   2. How do you get there?

4. **Emergencies**
   ▶ *Work in a group. Make a list of four emergency situations to call 911.* ▶ *Read your list to the class.*
   1. _____
   2. _____
   3. _____
   4. _____

5. **Make a list!**
   ▶ *Answer the questions with your class.* ▶ *Write a list on the board.*
   1. What do you do when you go the bank?
   2. What do you do when you go to the post office?
   3. What do you like about your neighborhood?
   4. When do you call 911?

ASSESSMENT

PART 1: Questions

▶ *Write questions to ask a classmate.*

1. Your neighborhood: _____

2. Your neighbors: _____

3. Around town: _____

4. The post office: _____

5. The bank: _____

6. A 911 call: _____

PART 2: Speaking

▶ *Work with a partner.* ▶ *Ask and answer your questions from Part 1.*

PART 3: Listening

🎧 ▶ *Listen.* ▶ *Circle a or b.**

1. a. About three weeks.
   b. Across the street.

2. a. Go straight past the school. It's on the right.
   b. On the corner of Central Street and Lake Avenue.

3. a. Yes, they are.
   b. Yes. I'd like to cash this check.

4. a. It's on Pine Avenue next to the bank.
   b. It takes about three days.

5. a. I'm calling to report a robbery.
   b. I'd like to make a deposit.

6. a. To New York.
   b. Express Mail.

PART 4: Writing

▶ *Write a conversation for this picture.*

OPERATOR: _____

CALLER: _____

OPERATOR: _____

CALLER: _____

OPERATOR: _____

CALLER: _____

OPERATOR: _____

* Answers are on p. 181.

UNIT 6
SHOPPING

PREVIEW

Preview Questions

▶ *Read the questions. What can you answer?*

1. What kind of store do you see in the picture?
2. What is on sale?
3. What are the people doing?
4. What are they saying?

Conversation Tip

▶ *Read the Conversation Tip.* ▶ *Practice with a partner.*

Repeat the question words when you don't understand what someone says.

A: Where can I get a cup of coffee?
B: Try Café International.
A: Excuse me. **Where**?
B: Café International.

A: How much are these shoes?
B: They're $39.99.
A: Excuse me. **How much**?
B: $39.99.
A: Thanks.

Conversation Chant: At the Shopping Mall

🎧 ▶ *Listen.* ▶ *Listen and repeat.* ▶ *Chant with your class.*

I need a notebook.

Try the stationery store.

I need a hammer.

Try the hardware store.

I need a cell phone and an i-Pod, too.

The electronics store is the store for you!

I want a basketball.

Try the sporting goods store.

I want a saxophone.

Try the music store.

I need a bright red T-shirt, extra small.

You'll find it all at the shopping mall!

Shopping at the Mall

1. At the mall

🎧 ▸ *Match the numbers and the words.** ▸ *Then listen and repeat.* ▸ *Add words.*

_____ a. coffee shop		_____ f. jewelry store		_____ k. stationery store	
_____ b. department store		_____ g. men's clothing store		_____ l. toy store	
_____ c. drugstore		_____ h. music store		_____ m. women's clothing store	
_____ d. electronics store		_____ i. shoe store		n. _____	
_____ e. hardware store		_____ j. sporting goods store		o. _____	

* Answers are on p. 181.

2. What can you get there?

▸ *Answer the questions with your class.*

1. What stores are in this mall?

2. What can you get at each store?

3. What's the name of the store?

▸ *Work with a partner.* ▸ *Write names for the stores in the picture.* ▸ *Tell the class.*

4. Ask directions at the mall

🎧 ▸ *Listen and repeat.* ▸ *Work with a partner.* ▸ *Write a conversation at the mall.* ▸ *Ask directions.* ▸ *Present your role play to the class.*

SHOPPER: Where can I get lunch?

HARRY: Try Carol's Café.

SHOPPER: Sorry, where?

HARRY: Carol's Café. It's on the 2nd level, next to the hardware store.

5. How about you?

▸ *Work with a partner.* ▸ *Ask and answer the questions.*

1. Where do you shop for:

a. clothing? _____

b. shoes? _____

c. stationery? _____

d. electronics? _____

e. jewelry? _____

f. toys? _____

g. sporting goods? _____

h. CDs? _____

2. What stores do you recommend? What can you buy there?

_____

Use your English!

▸ *With your conversation partner, visit a mall or shopping center.* ▸ *Find out what kinds of stores there are.* ▸ *Make a list.* ▸ *Report to the class.*

Lesson 2 Buying Shoes

1. At the shoe store

🎧 ▶ *Match the numbers and the words.** ▶ *Then listen and repeat.* ▶ *Add words.*

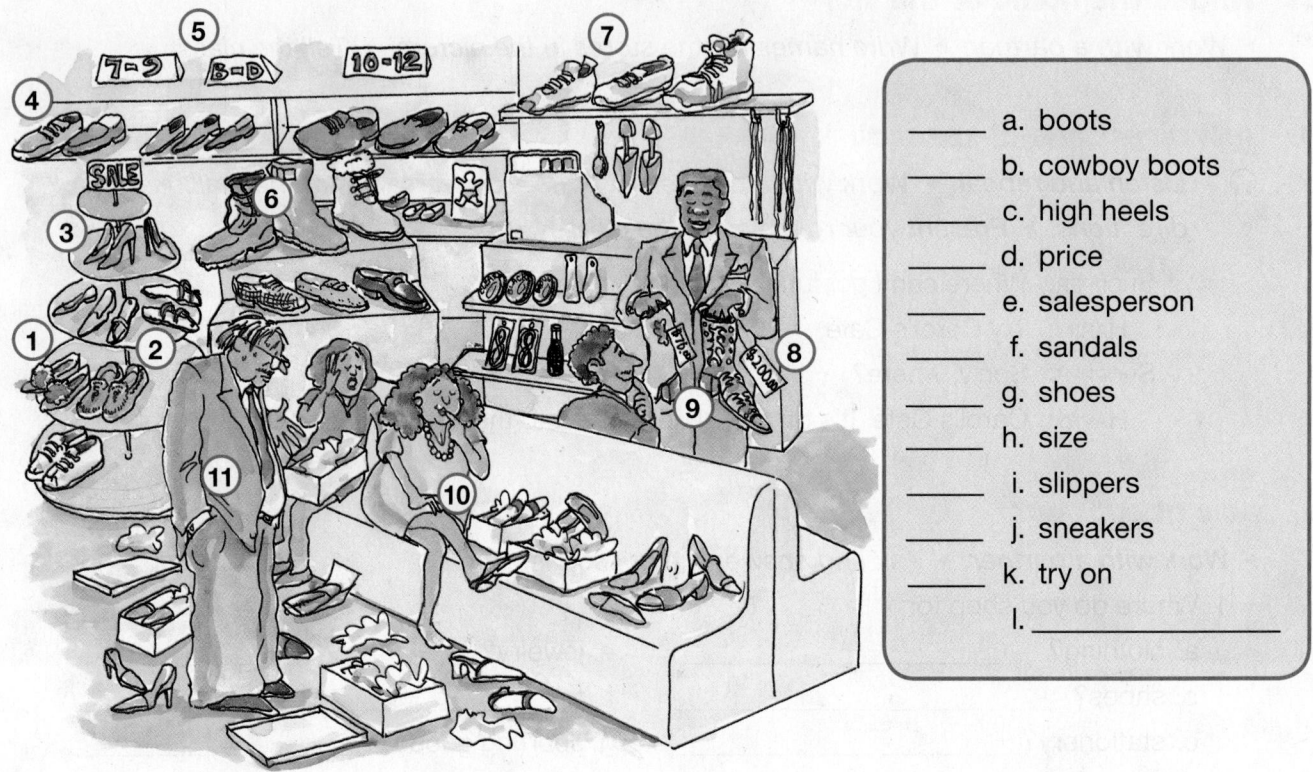

_____ a. boots
_____ b. cowboy boots
_____ c. high heels
_____ d. price
_____ e. salesperson
_____ f. sandals
_____ g. shoes
_____ h. size
_____ i. slippers
_____ j. sneakers
_____ k. try on
_____ l. _____

2. What's happening?

▶ *Answer the questions with your class.*

1. What is the woman shopping for? Does she like the shoes she is trying on? How is her friend feeling? How is the salesperson feeling?

2. What is the man shopping for? Does he like the boots he sees? What is he thinking?

3. How about you?

▶ *Work with a partner.* ▶ *Ask and answer the questions.*

1. What size shoes do you wear?

2. What kinds of shoes do you wear? What colors?

3. What are your favorite shoes?

* Answers are on p. 181.

4. What size do you wear?

🎧 ▶ *Listen and repeat.* ▶ *Practice with a partner.*

SALESPERSON: Can I help you?

CUSTOMER: Yes. I'm looking for cowboy boots.

SALESPERSON: What size do you wear?

CUSTOMER: Ten.

SALESPERSON: Excuse me? What size?

CUSTOMER: Size ten.

SALESPERSON: How about these boots?
They're on sale for $70.

CUSTOMER: Can I try them on?

SALESPERSON: Certainly.

---

5. Conversation Chant: Buying Shoes

🎧 ▶ *Listen.* ▶ *Listen and repeat.* ▶ *Chant with your class.*

Something comfortable,

Sneakers, sandals.

Something practical,

Sneakers, sandals.

Something reasonable,

Sneakers, sandals.

Something beautiful,

High- heeled shoes.

Something comfortable,

Sneakers, sandals.

Something practical,

Sneakers, sandals.

Something reasonable,

Sneakers, sandals.

Something beautiful,

Cowboy boots!

---

6. Find someone who. . .

▶ *Talk with your classmates.* ▶ *Ask the questions.* ▶ *Write names to complete the sentences.*

▶ *Report to the class.*

1. _____ wears size 6 shoes.
2. _____ wears size 10 shoes.
3. _____ never wears shoes at home.
4. _____ wears high heels to work.
5. _____ has more than five pairs of shoes.

Use your English!

▶ *Ask your conversation partner:* **Where do you shop for shoes? What stores do you recommend?** ▶ *Report the information to the class.*

Lesson 3 Shopping for Clothing

1. In the men's department

🎧 ▶ *Match the numbers and the words.* ▶ *Then listen and repeat.* ▶ *Add words.*

_____ a. extra large	_____ g. small	_____ m. vest
_____ b. gloves	_____ h. sports jacket	_____ n. wallet
_____ c. large	_____ i. sweat pants	o. _____
_____ d. long-sleeved shirt	_____ j. sweatshirt	p. _____
_____ e. medium	_____ k. tie	q. _____
_____ f. short-sleeved shirt	_____ l. underwear	r. _____

2. What can they buy?

▶ *Work with a partner.* ▶ *Complete the conversations.* ▶ *Present your role play to the class.*

1. SALESPERSON: May I help you?

   CUSTOMER: Yes, I'm looking for clothes for a job interview.

   SALESPERSON: _____

   CUSTOMER: _____

2. SALESPERSON: May I help you?

   CUSTOMER: I need a present for my father.

   SALESPERSON: _____

   CUSTOMER: _____

   * Answers are on p. 181.

3. In the women's department

_____ a. bathing suit	_____ e. nightgown	_____ i. sunglasses
_____ b. bathrobe	_____ f. panty hose	_____ j. underwear
_____ c. belt	_____ g. price tag	k. _____
_____ d. hat	_____ h. skirt	l. _____

4. What's in the picture?

▶ *Close your books and make a list of all the clothing you remember.* ▶ *Work in a group.*

▶ *Compare your lists.*

5. Role play

▶ *Work with a partner.* ▶ *Write a conversation between a customer and a salesperson in a clothing store.* ▶ *Present your role play to the class.*

Use your English!

▶ *Ask your conversation partner:* **Where do you shop for men's clothing? Where do you shop for women's clothing? What stores do you recommend?** ▶ *Report the information to the class.*

Shopping for Jewelry

1. Jewelry

🎧 ▶ *Match the numbers and the words.** ▶ Then listen and repeat. ▶ Add words.*

_____ a. bracelet   _____ e. necklace   i. _____

_____ b. diamond ring   _____ f. ring   j. _____

_____ c. earrings   _____ g. silver

_____ d. gold   _____ h. watch

2. What's happening?

▶ *Answer the questions with your class.*

1. What is the young couple shopping for? How much does the young man want to spend? Which ring does the young woman want? What is the salesperson thinking?

2. What is the older couple shopping for? Why is the man so happy? Why is the woman so happy? What is the salesperson thinking?

3. What are the two women doing? What are they looking at? Are they buying something? What is the salesperson thinking?

3. Role play

▶ *Work in a group of three.* ▶ *Choose three people in the jewelry store picture.* ▶ *Write a conversation for the three people.* ▶ *Present your role play to the class.*

          * Answers are on p. 181.

4. What's your favorite piece of jewelry?

▶ *Ask four classmates:* **What's your favorite piece of jewelry? Why do you like it?** ▶ *Write their names and their favorite jewelry.* ▶ *Report to the class.*

1. _____
   (Name)   (Favorite jewelry)

2. _____
   (Name)   (Favorite jewelry)

3. _____
   (Name)   (Favorite jewelry)

4. _____
   (Name)   (Favorite jewelry)

5. How many?

▶ *Work in a group.* ▶ *Ask the questions.* ▶ *Fill in the numbers.* ▶ *Compare your numbers with the class.*

1. How many classmates are wearing necklaces?	_____
2. How many are wearing watches?	_____
3. How many are wearing earrings?	_____
4. How many are wearing rings?	_____
5. How many are wearing bracelets?	_____

6. Who am I?

▶ *Write the accessories and colors you are wearing on a piece of paper.* ▶ *Fold your paper.*
▶ *Make a pile.* ▶ *Open one.* ▶ *Read it to the class.* ▶ *Guess who it is.*

Use your English!

▶ *Ask your conversation partner:* **What's your favorite piece of jewelry? Why?**
▶ *Do a survey of your friends:* Ask: **Where do you shop for jewelry? What stores do you recommend?** ▶ *Report your result to the class.*

Lesson 5 Sales and Advertisements

1. Sales and Advertisements

🎧 ▸ *Match the numbers and the sentences.* * ▸ *Then listen and repeat.*

_____ a. Rashid buys the car and drives it home.

_____ b. Rashid sees a car that he likes.

_____ c. Rashid sees an ad in the newspaper for used cars.

_____ d. The car breaks down on the way home.

2. Rashid's mistake

▸ *Answer the questions with your class.*

1. What mistake did Rashid make?

2. What can he do now?

3. What can he do next time?

3. What's happening?

▸ *Work with a partner.* ▸ *Tell Angela's story.*

4. How about you?

▸ *Work with a partner.* ▸ *Ask and answer the questions.*

1. Do you like to shop at sales? Why or why not?

2. What stores have good sales?

3. What time of year are there good sales?

4. Are there any good sales this week?

* Answers are on p. 181.

5. A raincheck

🎧 ▸ *Listen and repeat.* ▸ *Practice with a partner.*

BERTA: The towels are sold out. Can I get a raincheck?

SALESPERSON: Yes. Fill out this form. We can call you when more towels come in.

BERTA: Thanks.

6. What's on sale?

▸ *Ask and answer with a partner.*

1. What's on sale?
2. What's Berta doing?
3. What's a raincheck?
4. Do you buy sheets and towels on sale?

7. A yard sale

▸ *Work in a group.* ▸ *Answer the questions.*

1. What's for sale in this yard sale?
1. Do you like to go to yard sales? Why or why not?
2. What kinds of things can you buy at yard sales?
3. Can you find good deals at yard sales?
4. Are there many yard sales in your community?

8. Cross cultural exchange

▸ *Work in a group.* ▸ *Ask and answer the questions.* ▸ *Report to the class.*

1. Do people have yard sales in your country?
2. How do people sell personal items in your country?
3. What special sales do stores have in your country?
4. Are there rainchecks for sale items in your country?

Use your English!

▸ *Ask your conversation partner:* **Do you likes to shop at sales?** *Ask:* **What stores in your community have good sales?**

Lesson 6   Shopping in the 21st Century

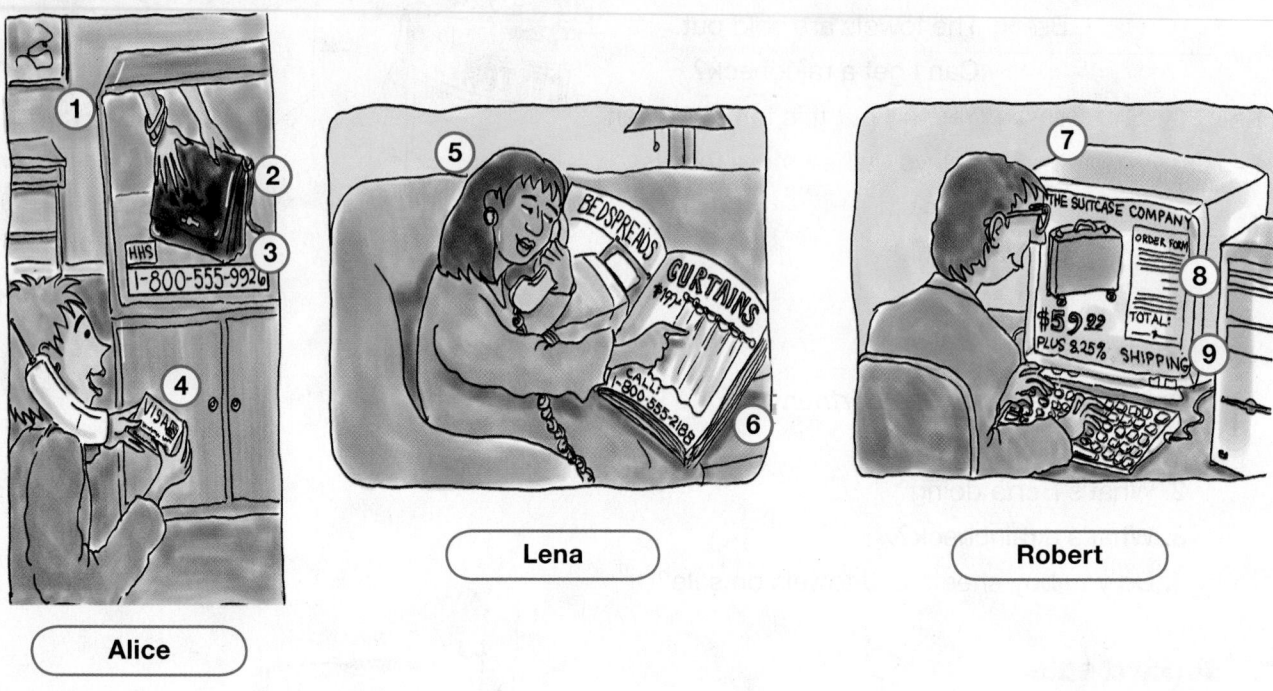

Alice

Lena

Robert

1. Shopping

🎧 ▶ *Match the numbers and the words.* ▶ *Then listen and repeat.*

_____ a. catalog	_____ d. order form	_____ g. telephone order
_____ b. credit card	_____ e. purse	_____ h. toll-free number
_____ c. home-shopping channel	_____ f. shop online	_____ i. Web site

2. How do they like to shop?

▶ *Answer the questions with your class.*

1. How does Alice like to shop? How does she pay for her purchases?

2. How does Lena like to shop? How does she pay for her purchases? Why does Lena like to shop at home?

3. How does Robert like to shop? How does he pay for his purchases? Why does Robert like to shop online?

* Answers are on p. 181.

3. How about you?

▶ *Work with a partner.* ▶ *Ask and answer the questions.*

1. Do you shop online? What do you buy?
2. Do you watch a home-shopping channel? Which one?
3. Do you look at catalogs? Which ones?
4. How do you pay for your purchases?
5. What's your favorite way to shop?

4. What are they saying?

▶ *Match the questions and the answers.* * ▶ *Compare your answers with a partner.*

_____ 1. Can I help you?		a. 2424-2727-9393-0098, 06/09
_____ 2. What's the item number?		b. Yes. I'd like to place an order.
_____ 3. How would you like to pay?		c. Black.
_____ 4. What's the credit card number and expiration date?		d. With a credit card.
_____ 5. What color do you want?		e. Number 88753E.

5. Role play

▶ *Work with a partner.* ▶ *Write a telephone conversation between Alice (or Lena) and a customer service representative.* ▶ *Present your role play to the class.*

6. A shopping survey

▶ *Work in a group.* ▶ *Ask and answer the questions.* ▶ *Count the answers and report to the class.*

HOW OFTEN DO YOU . . .	OFTEN	SOMETIMES	NEVER
1. watch the home-shopping channel?			
2. use a credit card online?			
3. give your credit card number on the phone?			
5. buy clothing from catalogs?			
6. compare prices before you buy something?			

Use your English!

▶ *With your conversation partner, watch a home-shopping channel.* **What items are being sold?** ▶ *Report to the class.*

LISTENING PRACTICE

1. Questions and answers

🎧 ▶ *Listen.* ▶ *Circle a or b.* *

1. a. Yes. I'd like to place an order.
   b. Try the sporting goods store.
2. a. $125.00.
   b. Size 11.
3. a. It's too small.
   b. Large.
4. a. Size 9.
   b. They're too big.

5. a. Number 78892.
   b. 07/08.
6. a. With a credit card.
   b. $20.00
7. a. I recommend Star Electronics.
   b. $6.00.
8. a. It's a yard sale.
   b. Yes. I'm looking for a bathing suit.

2. Where are they?

🎧 ▶ *Listen.* ▶ *Circle a or b.* *

CONVERSATION 1

Where are they?

a. In a clothing store.

b. In a jewelry store.

CONVERSATION 2

Where are they?

a. In a shoe store.

b. In a clothing store.

CONVERSATION 3

Where are they?

a. In a mall.

b. At home.

CONVERSATION 4

What are they doing?

a. They're shopping online.

b. They're shopping with the home-shopping channel.

3. Placing an order

🎧 ▶ *Look at the catalog item and the credit card.* ▶ *Listen to the questions and write the answers.*

1. _____
2. _____
3. _____
4. _____
5. _____
6. _____

warm winter sweater

Colors:
red, blue, green, black   #20987
Sizes: S. M. L. XL $29

* Answers are on p. 181.

REVIEW

1. What kind of store is it?

▶ *Think of a store.* ▶ *What can you get there?* ▶ *Write three items on a piece of paper.* ▶ *Fold your paper.* ▶ *Make a pile.* ▶ *Open one.* ▶ *Read it to the class.* ▶ *Guess what store.*

2. What's your partner wearing?

▶ *Work with a partner.* ▶ *Look at your partner's clothing.* ▶ *Sit back-to-back.* ▶ *List everything your partner is wearing.* ▶ *How many details are correct?* ▶ *Look at your a partner.* ▶ *Correct your list.*

3. What do people wear?

▶ *Work in a group.* ▶ *Answer the questions.* ▶ *Fill in the circles.* ▶ *Report to the class.*

1. What do women wear?
2. What do men wear?
3. What do both women and men wear?

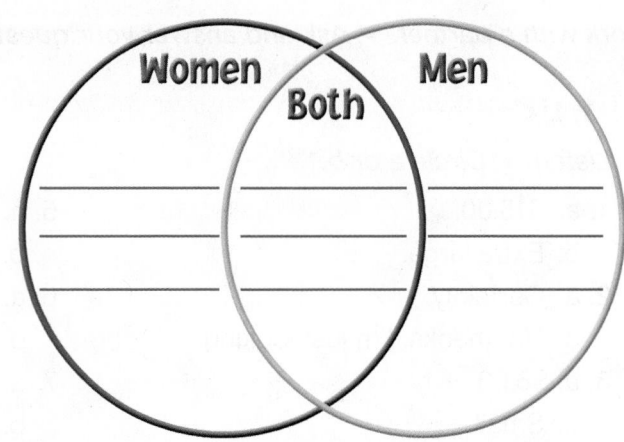

4. Shopping

▶ *Work with a partner.* ▶ *Complete the conversations.* ▶ *Present your role plays to another pair of students.*

1.   CUSTOMER: Where can I get a tie?
    SALESPERSON: Try _____
    CUSTOMER: Excuse me. _____
    SALESPERSON: _____

2. SALESPERSON: What size shoes do you wear?
    CUSTOMER: _____
    SALESPERSON: Excuse me. _____
    CUSTOMER: _____

ASSESSMENT

PART 1: Questions

▶ *Write questions that these people can ask.*

1. A salesperson: _____

_____

2. A customer at a store: _____

_____

3. A customer placing an order on the phone: _____

_____

4. A customer-service representative: _____

_____

PART 2: Speaking

▶ *Work with a partner.* ▶ *Ask and answer your questions from Part 1.*

PART 3: Listening

🎧 ▶ *Listen.* ▶ *Circle a or b.**

1. a. $15.00.
   b. Extra large.
2. a. Certainly.
   b. No, thanks. I'm just looking.
3. a. $6.00.
   b. Small.
4. a. Number 885761.
   b. 10/09.

5. a. Yes, I'm looking for a green sweater.
   b. Yes. The fitting rooms are over there.
6. a. It's too big.
   b. Size 10.
7. a. Yes, I'm looking for a green sweater.
   b. With my *Express* credit card.
8. a. Try the shoe store on Level 1.
   b. Try the jewelry store on Level 2.

PART 4: Writing

▶ *Write conversations for these pictures.*

1. SALESPERSON: _____

   RASHID: _____

   SALESPERSON: _____

   RASHID: _____

2. CUSTOMER-SERVICE REPRESENTATIVE: _____

   LENA: _____

   CUSTOMER-SERVICE REPRESENTATIVE: _____

   LENA: _____

UNIT 7
YOUR CALENDAR

PREVIEW

Preview Questions

▶ *Read the questions.* ▶ *What can you answer?*

1. Where are the people in the first picture? In the second picture?
2. What's the weather like in the pictures?
3. What months do you think the pictures show?
4. What seasons do the pictures show?

Conversation Tip

▶ *Read the Conversation Tip.* ▶ *Practice with a partner.*

Give extra information when you answer a question.

A: Where were you yesterday?
B: I was at the mall. **I bought a new coat.**

A: Will you be home tonight?
B: No, I won't. **I have to work tonight.**

Conversation Chant: A Surprise Party

🎧 ▶ *Listen.* ▶ *Listen and repeat.* ▶ *Chant with your class.*

Birthday cake,   Blow out the candles, pink and blue.

   Birthday presents,   It's a birthday partyfor you!

Party hats,   SURPRISE!!!

   Paper plates.

Months, Years, and Birthdays

JANUARY	FEBRUARY	MARCH	APRIL
MAY	JUNE	JULY	AUGUST
SEPTEMBER	OCTOBER	NOVEMBER	DECEMBER

1. Months and years

🎧 ▶ *Listen and repeat.* ▶ *Review numbers on page 169.* ▶ *Answer the questions with your class.*

1. What month and year is it now?

2. What was last month? What was last year?

3. What will next month be? What will next year be?

4. When was the first day of your class?

5. When is the last day of your class?

2. When's your birthday?

🎧 ▶ *Listen and repeat.* ▶ *Practice with a partner.*

CHER: What year were you born, Sue?

SUE: I was born in 1976. How about you, Cher? When were you born?

CHER: In 1978. And when's your birthday?

SUE: March 2nd. When's yours?

CHER: October 23rd.

3. How old . . . ?

▶ *Answer the questions with your class.*

1. How old is Cher now? How old is Sue?

2. How old will Cher be in 2020? How old will Sue be?

3. When is Cher's birthday? And Sue's?

4. Harry's surprise party

🎧 ▸ *Match the numbers and the words.** ▸ Then listen and repeat.* ▸ *Add words.*

_____	a. birthday cake
_____	b. birthday party
_____	c. candles
_____	d. hiding
_____	e. horn
_____	f. paper plates
_____	g. party hats
_____	h. presents
_____	i. punch
_____	j. refreshments
_____	k. surprised
	l. _____
	m. _____

5. What's happening?

🎧 ▸ *Listen and repeat.* ▸ *Practice with two partners.*

FRIENDS: Surprise! Happy birthday, Harry! Are you surprised?

HARRY: Wow! Yes! Unbelievable!

FRIENDS: Come in, Harry. Open your presents. Have some refreshments.

6. How about you?

▸ *Work with a partner.* ▸ *Ask and answer the questions.*

1. Do you like birthday parties?
2. What do you like to do on your birthday?
3. Where were you last year on your birthday?
4. How do people celebrate birthdays in your country?

7. Make a birthday card!

▸ *Write your name on a piece of paper.*

▸ *Make a pile.* ▸ *Open one.* ▸ *Make a birthday card for the name on your paper.*

▸ *Give the birthday card to your classmate.*

Use your English!

▸ *Tell your conversation partner where you buy birthday cards in your neighborhood.*

Lesson 2 Dates and Holidays

1. Holidays in the United States

🎧 ▸ *Match the numbers and the words.* ▸ *Then listen and repeat.* ▸ *Add words.*

_____ a. chocolates   _____ f. hearts   _____ k. trick or treat

_____ b. Christmas tree   _____ g. New Year's Eve   _____ l. turkey

_____ c. costumes   _____ h. noisemaker   m. _____

_____ d. family dinner   _____ i. parade   n. _____

_____ e. fireworks   _____ j. Santa Claus

2. Celebrating holidays

▸ *Answer the questions with your class.*

1. What are the dates of these holidays? When is Thanksgiving this year?

2. How are people in the pictures celebrating these holidays?

3. Do you celebrate any of these holidays? Which one(s)?

4. What holidays do people celebrate in your country?

   * Answers are on p. 181.

3. Holiday greetings

▶ *Work with a partner.* ▶ *Write the holiday names next to the greetings.** ▶ *Add more greetings and holidays.* ▶ *Report to the class.*

1. I love you. _____
2. Trick or treat! _____
3. Happy Turkey Day! _____
4. Happy Fourth of July! _____
5. Have a great 2008! _____
6. _____ _____
7. _____ _____

4. Favorite holidays

▶ *Work in a group.* ▶ *Fill in the chart.* ▶ *Tell the class your favorites.*

NAME	FAVORITE HOLIDAY	FAVORITE HOLIDAY FOOD	FAVORITE HOLIDAY ACTIVITY

5. Holiday songs and greetings

▶ *Teach the class how to say* **Happy New Year** *in your language.* ▶ *Sing your favorite holiday song for the class.*

6. What's the holiday?

▶ *Write a holiday food, activity, or greeting on a piece of paper.* ▶ *Fold your paper.*
▶ *Make a pile.* ▶ *Open one.* ▶ *Read.* ▶ *Guess the holiday.*

Use your English!

▶ *With your conversation partner, find out:* **On what holidays are schools closed? How about banks, post offices, government offices, and stores?**
▶ *Report the information to the class.*

---

* Answers are on p. 181.

Lesson 3 Weather Report

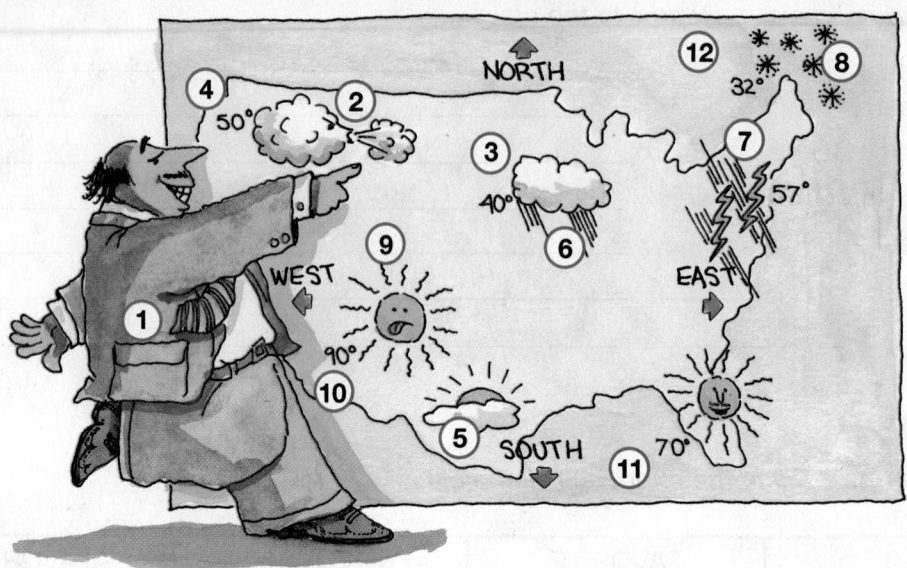

1. The weather

🎧 ► *Match the numbers and the words.** ► *Then listen and repeat.* ► *Add words.*

_____ a. cloudy	_____ f. meteorologist	_____ k. warm (70 degrees)
_____ b. cold (32 degrees)	_____ g. rainy	_____ l. windy
_____ c. cool (50 degrees)	_____ h. snowy	m. _____
_____ d. hot (90 degrees)	_____ i. sunny	n. _____
_____ e. lightning	_____ j. temperature	

2. The weather report

🎧 ► *Listen and read.* ► *Answer the questions with your class.*

METEOROLOGIST: Across the nation today we have a high temperature of 90 degrees in Arizona and a low of 32 in Maine. In the Midwest it's cloudy and rainy, with a high of 40 degrees. In the Northeast it's cold and snowy, and in the Northwest it's windy today.

1. What's the weather like in the Southwest? What's the temperature?
2. What's the weather like in the Southeast? What's the temperature?
3. What's the weather like in the Northeast? What's the temperature?
4. What's the weather like in the Northwest? What's the temperature?
5. What's your weather like today? What's the temperature?
6. What was your weather like yesterday? The day before yesterday?
7. What will it be like tomorrow? The day after tomorrow?

* Answers are on p. 181.

3. Celsius or Fahrenheit?

▶ *Write answers to the questions.* ▶ *Work in a group.* ▶ *Compare your answers.* ▶ *Check your answers with the class.*

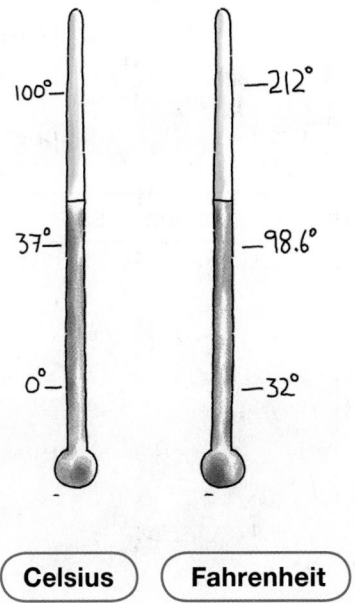

Celsius   Fahrenheit

Change from Celsius to Fahrenheit: $°F = \frac{9}{5}(°C) + 32$

Example: $20°C \times \frac{9}{5} = 36 + 32 = 68°F$

Change from Fahrenheit to Celsius: $°C = \frac{5}{9}(°F - 32)$

Example: $68°F - 32 = 36 \times \frac{5}{9} = 20°C$

1. The temperature is 10°C.
   What's the temperature in Fahrenheit? _____ °F*
2. The temperature is 86°F.
   What's the temperature in Celsius? _____ °C*
3. What are summer temperatures in your area?
   In Celsius? _____ °C   In Fahrenheit? _____ °F
4. What are winter temperatures in your area?
   In Celsius? _____ °C   In Fahrenheit? _____ °F

4. Tomorrow's weather forecast

🎧 ▶ *Listen and repeat.* ▶ *Practice with a partner.*

METEOROLOGIST: And now, here's our local forecast. Our weather here for the next two days will be *sunny, warm, and windy*. Tomorrow's high temperature will be *72 degrees*. The day after tomorrow will be the same.

5. Role play

▶ *Choose a date.* ▶ *Imagine you are a meteorologist.* ▶ *Write a weather report for your city for that date.* ▶ *Present your role play for the class.*

Use your English!

▶ *With your conversation partner, watch a weather report on TV.*
▶ *Take notes.* ▶ *Report to the class.*

Lesson 4   Good and Bad Weather

a sunny day

a rainy day

a windy day

a hailstorm

a snowy day

1. Weather

🎧 ▶ *Match the numbers and the words.* ▶ *Use some numbers more than once.** ▶ *Then listen and repeat.* ▶ *Add words.*

_____ a. blow	_____ f. sky	_____ k. thunder
_____ b. cloud	_____ g. snowstorm	_____ l. windy
_____ c. hail	_____ h. snowy	m. _____
_____ d. lightning	_____ i. sunny	n. _____
_____ e. rainy	_____ j. sunshine	

2. What's happening in the pictures?

▶ *Work with a partner.* ▶ *Match the titles of the pictures with the sentences below.**

▶ *Report to the class.*

1. It's snowing. A man is shoveling snow. _____

2. There's thunder, lightning, and hail. _____

3. The wind is blowing. A man and a horse are walking in the desert. _____

4. It's raining. A little boy is playing in the puddles. _____

5. The sun is shining. A man is lying under a tree. _____

       * Answers are on p. 182.

3. **Good weather/Bad weather**

▶ *Work with a partner.* ▶ *Ask and answer the questions.*

1. What is your favorite weather? Why?
2. What kind of weather don't you like? Why not?
3. Do you like the weather today? Why or why not?

4. **Find someone who . . .**

▶ *Talk to your classmates.* ▶ *Ask the questions.* ▶ *Write names to complete the sentences.*

▶ *Report to the class.*

1. _____ likes snowy days.
2. _____ likes to read on rainy days.
3. _____ likes to be outside in all kinds of weather.
4. _____ feels happy on sunny days.
5. _____ likes windy days.

5. **Conversation Chant: Sailors Love the Wind**

🎧 ▶ *Listen.* ▶ *Listen and repeat.* ▶ *Chant with your class.*

Sailors love the wind,

The sound of the wind

Strong wind on the sail.

Sailors love the wind.

They don't like the rain,

Thunder, lightning, or hail.

Skiers love the snow,

Swimmers love the sun,

But if you're a sailor,

The wind is fun.

Use your English!

▶ *With your conversation partner, find places in the world with the same weather as your country.* ▶ *Report to the class.*

Lesson 5　The Seasons

spring

summer

fall

winter

1. The seasons

🎧 ▶ *Match the numbers and the words.* ▶ *Then listen and repeat.* ▶ *Add words.*

What are the things and places?	What do people like to do?	
_____ a. apple cider	_____ f. plant a garden	k. _____
_____ b. beach	_____ g. play volleyball	l. _____
_____ c. bird	_____ h. rake leaves	m. _____
_____ d. nest	_____ i. shovel snow	n. _____
_____ e. pumpkin	_____ j. go skating	

2. Spring, summer, fall, winter

▶ *Answer the questions with your class.*

1. What do you see in the picture of spring? In the picture of summer? Of fall? Of winter?

2. What are the people doing in each picture?

3. What's the weather like in each picture?

3. How about you?

▶ *Work with a partner.* ▶ *Ask and answer the questions.*

1. How many seasons are there where you live? What are they?

2. What is the weather like in each season?

3. What months are in each season?

4. What do people like to do in each season? What do they eat and drink in each season?

5. How many seasons are there in your country? What are they?

4. Find someone who . . .

▶ *Talk to your classmates.* ▶ *Ask the questions.* ▶ *Write names to complete the sentences.*

▶ *Report to the class.*

1. _____ rakes leaves in the fall.
2. _____ likes to plant a garden in the spring.
3. _____ goes to the beach in the summer.
4. _____ shovels snow in the winter.
5. _____ sometimes goes skating.

5. How about you?

▶ *Work with a partner.* ▶ *Ask and answer the questions.*

1. What do you like about this season now?

2. What season were you born in? Do you like that season?

3. Where were you last spring? Last summer? Last fall? Last winter?

4. What do you like to eat and drink in each season?

6. Your favorite season

▶ *Ask four classmates:* **What's your favorite season? Why?** ▶ *Write the answers.*

▶ *Report to the class.*

	NAME	FAVORITE SEASON	WHY?
1.	_____	_____	_____
2.	_____	_____	_____
3.	_____	_____	_____
4.	_____	_____	_____

Use your English!

▶ *Ask your conversation partner:* **What do you do in the spring? In the summer? In the fall? In the winter?**

Lesson 6   Taking a Trip

1. Taking a trip

🎧 ▶ **Match the numbers and the words.*** ▶ **Listen and repeat.** ▶ **Add words.**

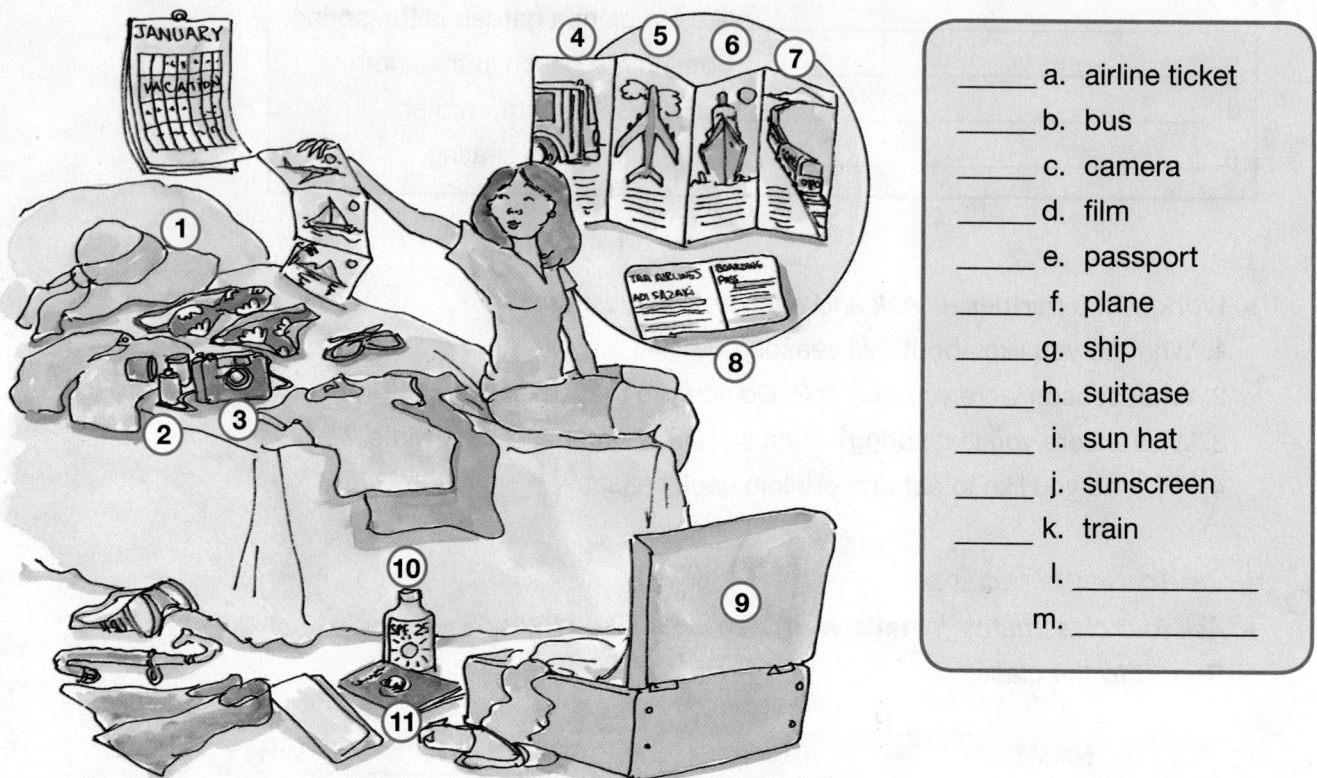

_____	a. airline ticket
_____	b. bus
_____	c. camera
_____	d. film
_____	e. passport
_____	f. plane
_____	g. ship
_____	h. suitcase
_____	i. sun hat
_____	j. sunscreen
_____	k. train
	l. _____
	m. _____

2. What's in the picture?

▶ **Answer the questions with your class.**

1. What is Yumiko packing for her trip?
2. How is she traveling? How do you know?
3. Where do you think she is going?

3. What are they saying?

🎧 ▶ **Listen and repeat.** ▶ **Practice with a partner.**

A: Where are you going on your trip, Yumiko?

B: I'm going to Puerto Rico. My flight leaves at 7 A.M.

A: What are you going to do there?

B: I'm going swimming and sightseeing.

A: It sounds great, Yumiko. Have a wonderful time.

B: Thanks.

4. Role play

▸ *Work with a partner.* ▸ *Look at the maps on pages 161-167.* ▸ *Choose a country.*

▸ *Write a conversation about a trip.* ▸ *Present your role play to the class.*

5. Who is it?

▸ *Where do you want to go on a trip?* ▸ *Write the name of the place on a piece of paper.*

▸ *Fold your paper.* ▸ *Make a pile.* ▸ *Open one.* ▸ *Read.* ▸ *Guess who wrote it.*

6. Packing ABC game

▸ *Work in a group.* ▸ *Take turns: Go through the alphabet from A to Z.* ▸ *Follow the example below.* ▸ *Share your ideas with the class.*

I'm taking a trip, and I'm packing an **a**irline ticket.

I'm taking a trip, and I'm packing a **b**athing suit.

I'm taking a trip, and I'm packing a **c**_____ .

---

7. Conversation Chant: Taking a Trip

🎧 ▸ *Listen.* ▸ *Listen and repeat.* ▸ *Chant with your class.*

Are you ready to go?

　　Yes, I am.

Did you pack your sunhat?

　　Yes, I did.

Are your bags all packed?

　　Yes, they are.

Where's your computer?

　　It's in the car.

Do you have your ticket?

　　Yes I do. It's in my wallet with my
　　credit cards, too.

Where's your passport ?

I don't know, but you don't

need a passport for Idaho.

Use your English!

▸ *Ask your conversation partner about a trip he or she wants to take.*

LISTENING PRACTICE

1. Holidays

🎧 ▶ *Listen.* ▶ *Circle a, b, or c.**

CONVERSATION 1

What holiday is it?

a. Thanksgiving

b. Halloween

c. Christmas

CONVERSATION 2

What holiday is it?

a. Independence Day

b. New Year's Day

c. Valentine's Day

CONVERSATION 3

What holiday is it?

a. Halloween

b. Christmas

c. New Year's Day

2. A weather report

🎧 ▶ *Listen.* ▶ *Circle a or b.**

1. What was the low temperature in Montana today?

   a. 29°   b. 19°

2. What will the weather be like tomorrow in the Southeast?

   a. Sunny and hot   b. Rainy and warm

3. What will the weather be like tomorrow in the West?

   a. Rainy   b. Cloudy and cool

4. What will the high temperature be here tomorrow?

   a. 56°   b. 88°

3. Where are they?

🎧 ▶ *Listen.* ▶ *Match the conversations with the pictures.* ▶ *Write the numbers.*

* Answers are on p. 182.

REVIEW

1. **Talking about the calendar**
   ▶ *Work with a partner.* ▶ *Answer the questions.*
   1. What's today's date?
   2. What was yesterday's date? The day before yesterday's? Last Tuesday's?
   3. What's tomorrow's date? The day after tomorrow's? Next Sunday's?

2. **What holiday is it?**
   ▶ *Write answers to the questions on a piece of paper.* ▶ *Fold your paper.* ▶ *Make a pile.*
   ▶ *Open one.* ▶ *Read.* ▶ *Guess what holiday.*
   Think of a holiday.
   1. What season is it in?
   2. What do people do for that holiday?

3. **Weather report**
   ▶ *Work with a partner.* ▶ *Write a weather report for today and a forecast for tomorrow.*
   ▶ *Present your weather report and forecast to the class.*

4. **Make a list!**
   ▶ *Work in a group.* ▶ *Choose a place and a month for a trip.* ▶ *Make a list of things to pack*
   ▶ *for your trip.* ▶ *Share your ideas with the class.*

5. **How about you?**
   ▶ *Work with a partner.* ▶ *Ask and answer the questions.* ▶ *Tell the class about your partner.*
   1. When's your birthday?
   2. Where were you the day before yesterday?   Where will you be tomorrow?
   3. What's your favorite weather?
   4. What's your favorite holiday?

ASSESSMENT

PART 1: Questions

▶ *Write questions to ask a classmate.*

1. Dates: _____

2. Birthdays: _____

3. Holidays: _____

4. Weather: _____

5. Seasons: _____

6. Taking a trip: _____

PART 2: Speaking

▶ *Work with a partner.* ▶ *Ask and answer your questions from Part 1.*

PART 3: Listening

🎧 ▶ *Listen.* ▶ *Circle a or b.* *

1. a. Yes, it is.
   b. Yes, it was a rainy day.
2. a. It's on October 27th.
   b. I think it's November 24th.
3. a. In July, 1985.
   b. I was born in Peru.

4. a. Yes, I am. I'm going to Hawaii in February.
   b. I don't think so. But maybe I'll go to Europe in the fall.
5. a. It's Monday.
   b. It's June 2nd.
6. a. Because the weather there is warm this time of the year.
   b. Because I don't want to be cold.

PART 4: Writing

▶ *Write conversations for these pictures.*

A: _____

B: _____

A: _____

A: _____

B: _____

C: _____

UNIT 8
YOUR HEALTH

PREVIEW

Preview Questions

▶ *Read the questions.* ▶ *What can you answer?*

1. Where are the people in the picture?
2. What are they doing?
3. What are they saying?

Conversation Tip

▶ *Read the Conversation Tip.* ▶ *Practice with a partner.*

Express your feelings when you hear good news or bad news.

A: How are you doing?
B: Not so great. I have a terrible cold.
A: **I'm sorry to hear that.** I hope you feel better soon.
B: Thanks.

A: How are you feeling?
B: Great! My cold is gone.
A: **I'm glad to hear that.**
B: Thanks.

Conversation Chant: What's Wrong with Joe?

🎧 ▶ *Listen.* ▶ *Listen and repeat.* ▶ *Chant with your class.*

What's wrong with Joe?

I don't know.

He's got a headache, backache,

stomachache, too.

It sounds like he might be getting the flu.

How about Jill? Is she feeling OK?

She was feeling fine when I saw her

yesterday.

How about Danny? Is he all right?

He called a doctor late last night.

What did the doctor do? What did she say?

She said, "Take two aspirin,

and you'll be OK."

Staying Healthy

1. The human body

🎧 ▶ *Match the numbers and the words.** ▶ *Then listen and repeat.* ▶ *Add words.*

_____ a. ankle	_____ f. foot	_____ k. neck
_____ b. arm	_____ g. hand	_____ l. toes
_____ c. back	_____ h. head	m. _____
_____ d. elbow	_____ i. knee	n. _____
_____ e. fingers	_____ j. leg	

2. What's this?

▶ *Work in a group.* ▶ *Point to a part of the body. Ask:* **What's this?** *or* **What are these?**

▶ *Have the group name the part of the body.*

* Answers are on p. 182.

3. Healthy habits

▶ *Work in a group.* ▶ *Answer the questions.* ▶ *Report to the class.*

1. What is healthy food? Give three examples.
2. What is a good way to exercise? Give three examples.
3. How much sleep is *enough* sleep? Six hours a night? Eight hours a night?

eat healthy food

sleep enough

exercise

4. Do you have healthy habits?

▶ *Work in a group.* ▶ *Ask and answer the questions.* ▶ *Report to the class.*

HOW OFTEN DO YOU . . .	ONCE A WEEK	THREE TIMES A WEEK	EVERY DAY OR EVERY NIGHT
1. sleep eight hours a night?	_____	_____	_____
2. exercise?	_____	_____	_____
3. eat fruit?	_____	_____	_____
4. eat vegetables?	_____	_____	_____

5. Conversation Chant: Exercise Every Day!

🎧 ▶ *Listen.* ▶ *Listen and repeat.* ▶ *Chant with your class.*

Walking, running,

Biking, hiking.

Exercise, every day.

Fruit and vegetables,

Lots of vegetables.

Eat well, every day.

Plenty of rest, lots of rest,

Sleep well, every night.

Plenty of exercise

Every day.

Follow your dreams.

Do what you love!

> ### Use your English!
>
> ▶ *Ask your conversation partner:* **How many hours do you sleep a night? How often do you exercise?** ▶ *Report to the class.*

Lesson 2 What's the Matter?

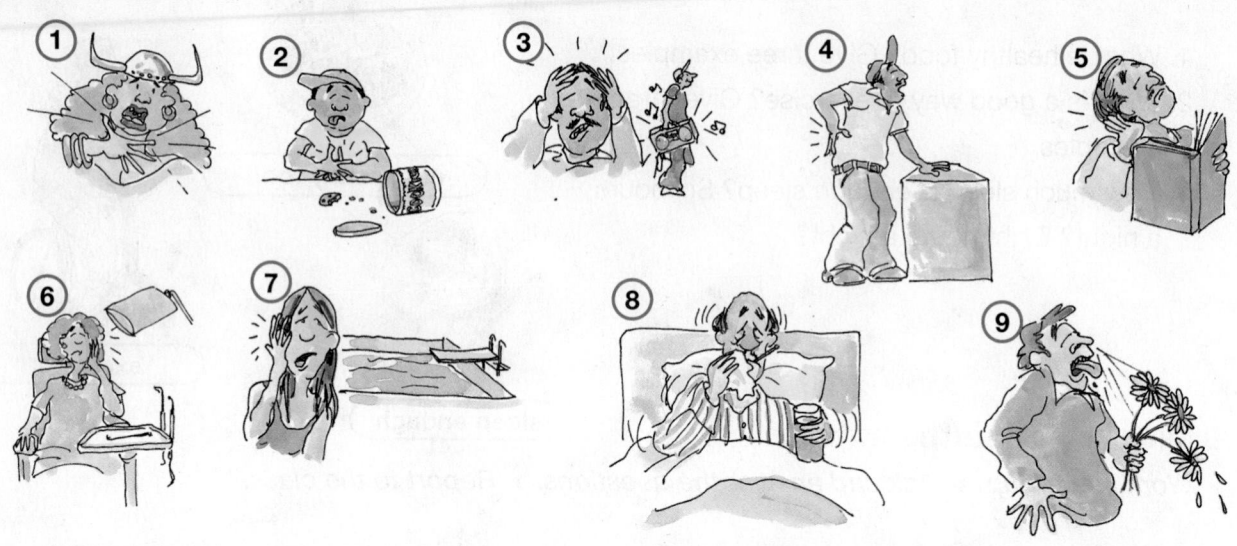

1. Ailments

🎧 ▶ *Match the numbers and the words.** ▶ Use some numbers more than once. ▶ Then listen and repeat.* ▶ *Add words.*

_____ a. allergies	_____ f. a headache	_____ k. a toothache
_____ b. a backache	_____ g. a runny nose	l. _____
_____ c. a cold	_____ h. a sore throat	m. _____
_____ d. an earache	_____ i. a stiff neck	n. _____
_____ e. a fever	_____ j. a stomachache	

2. What's the matter?

▶ *Work with your class.* ▶ *Review* **Inside the Body** *on page 171.* ▶ *Act out an ailment.*
▶ *Have the class guess the ailment.*

3. How are they doing?

🎧 ▶ *Listen and repeat.* ▶ *Practice with a partner.*

1. A: How are you doing?
   B: Not so great.
   A: Oh? What's the matter?
   B: I have a sore throat.
   A: I'm sorry to hear that. I hope
      you feel better soon.
   B: Thanks.

2. A: How are you feeling?
   B: Great! My stomachache
      went away.
   A: I'm glad to hear that.
   B: Thanks.

* Answers are on p. 182.

4. How are you doing?

▶ *Ask four classmates:* **How are you doing?** ▶ *Report to the class.*

5. Making an appointment

🎧 ▶ *Match the questions and answers.** ▶ *Then listen and repeat.* ▶ *Practice the conversation with a partner.*

Receptionist

_____ 1. Doctor Barry's office. May I help you?

_____ 2. What's the reason for the appointment?

_____ 3. Do you have a fever?

_____ 4. How about this afternoon at 4:30?

_____ 5. Can I have your name, please?

Anna

a. That sounds good.

b. Yes. I'd like to make an appointment with the doctor.

c. I have a sore throat and a runny nose.

d. Anna Smith.

e. Yes. It's 101.

6. Role play

▶ *Work with a partner.* ▶ *Write a phone conversation between a receptionist and a patient.*

▶ *Present your role play to the class.*

Use your English!

▶ *With your conversation partner, use the Internet or your local telephone book.*

▶ *Find and write down the addresses and phone numbers for three doctors in your neighborhood.* ▶ *Report the information to the class.*

Lesson 3 The Drugstore

1. At the drugstore

🎧 ▶ *Match the numbers and the words.** ▶ *Then listen and repeat.* ▶ *Add words.*

_____ a. antacid	_____ f. diapers	_____ k. tissues
_____ b. aspirin	_____ g. makeup	_____ l. vitamins
_____ c. bandages	_____ h. nail polish	m. _____
_____ d. cold medicine	_____ i. pharmacist	n. _____
_____ e. cough syrup	_____ j. sunscreen	o. _____

2. What can you buy there?

▶ *Answer the questions with your class.*

1. What can you get at this drugstore?

2. What can you get at the drugstore in your neighborhood?

* Answers are on p. 182.

3. **What's in this medicine cabinet?**

▶ *Ask and answer with your partner.*

1. What's in this medicine cabinet?
2. Do you have any of these items at home?
3. Do you have a medicine cabinet at home?
   What's in it?

4. **What items are necessary in a medicine cabinet?**

▶ *Work with a group. List ten items that are necessary in a medicine cabinet.*

▶ *Report to the class.*

1. _____
2. _____
3. _____
4. _____
5. _____
6. _____
7. _____
8. _____
9. _____
10. _____

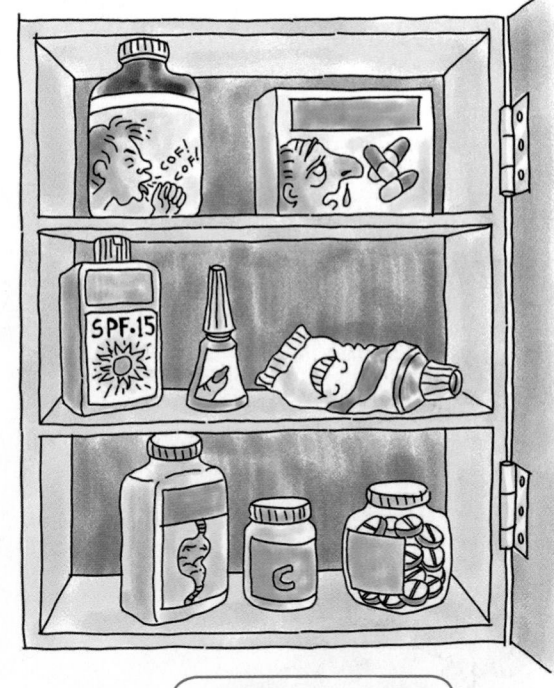

medicine cabinet

5. **What do you recommend for headaches?**

🎧 ▶ *Listen and repeat.* ▶ *Practice with a partner.*

PHARMACIST: May I help you?

CUSTOMER: Yes. I have a headache. What do you recommend?

PHARMACIST: Try Panax aspirin. It really works.

CUSTOMER: Thanks.

6. **Role play**

▶ *Work with a partner.* ▶ *Write a conversation between a pharmacist and a customer.*

▶ *Present your role play to the class.*

Use your English!

▶ *Ask your conversation partner:* **What medicine do you recommend for a headache? For a stomachache? For a cold? For a sore throat?** ▶ *Report to the class.*

Lesson 4 Going to the Doctor

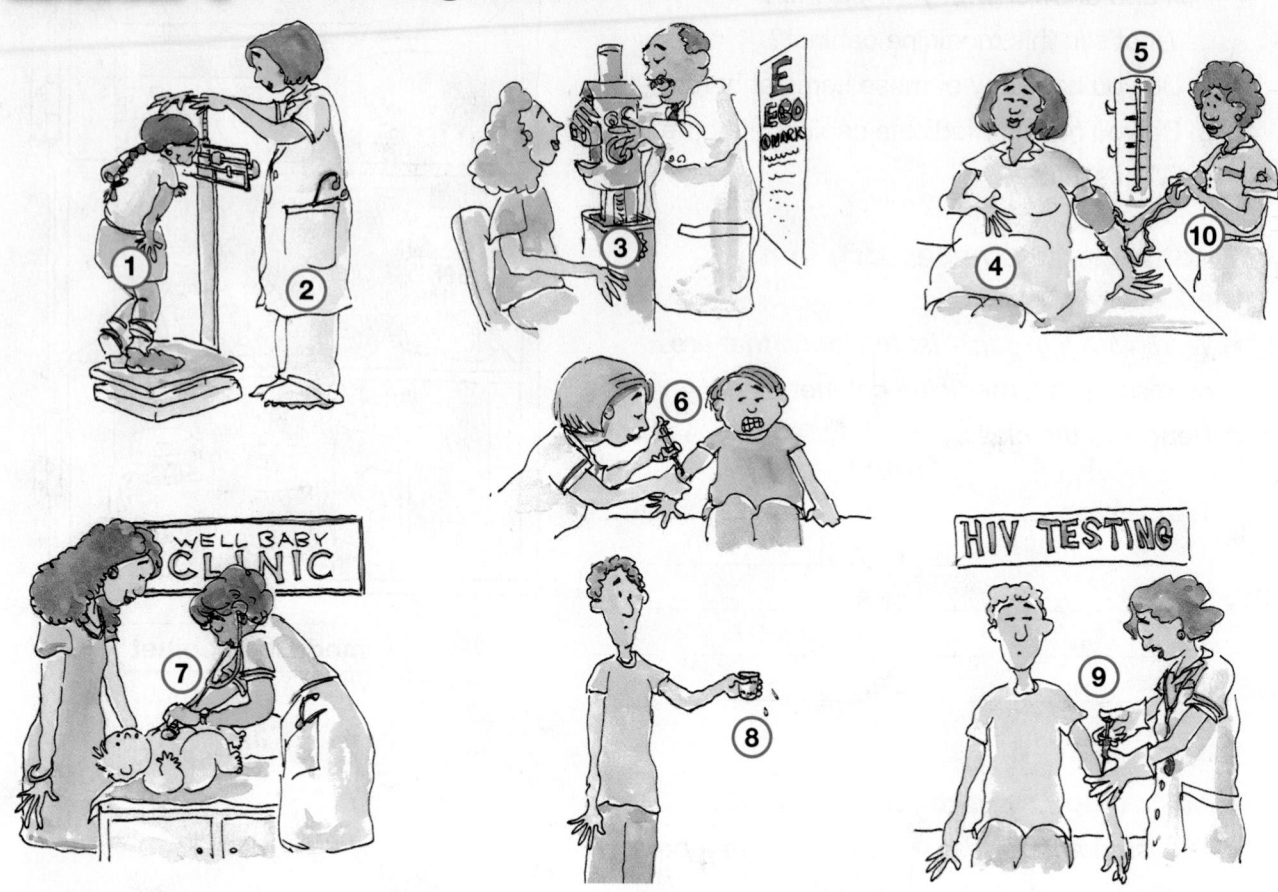

1. Doctor visits

🎧 ▶ *Match the numbers and the words.* ▶ *Then listen and repeat.* ▶ *Add words.*

_____ a. blood pressure	_____ f. nurse	k. _____
_____ b. blood test	_____ g. patient	l. _____
_____ c. doctor	_____ h. stethoscope	m. _____
_____ d. eye exam	_____ i. urine sample	
_____ e. injection	_____ j. weight	

2. What are they doing?

▶ *Answer the questions with your class.*

1. What are the people doing?
2. When do you go to the doctor?

     * Answers are on p. 182.

3. You should see the doctor

▶ *Work with a partner.* ▶ *Complete the conversations.*

▶ *Present one of the role plays to the class.*

1. A: My allergies are terrible this month
   B: You should see your allergist!
2. A: I can't read the newspaper. The words are too small.
   B: You should see the _____
3. A: My baby has a fever.
   B: Take the baby to the _____
4. A: Uh-oh! I don't feel very well. I think the baby is coming!
   B: Call the _____

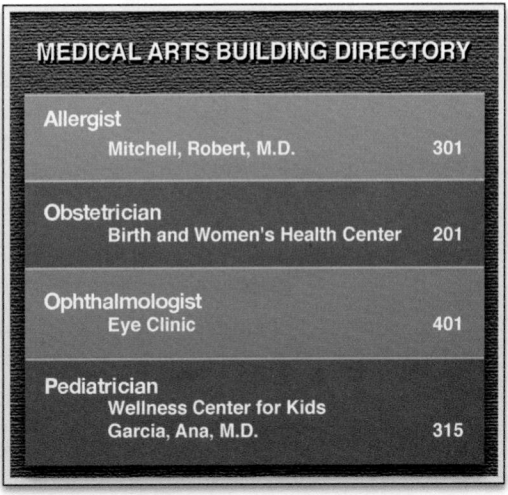

MEDICAL ARTS BUILDING DIRECTORY

Allergist	
Mitchell, Robert, M.D.	301
Obstetrician	
Birth and Women's Health Center	201
Ophthalmologist	
Eye Clinic	401
Pediatrician	
Wellness Center for Kids	
Garcia, Ana, M.D.	315

4. At the doctor's office

🎧 ▶ *Listen and repeat.* ▶ *Practice with a partner.*

PATIENT: I have an appointment with Dr. Mitchell.

RECEPTIONIST: What time is your appointment?

PATIENT: 2:15.

RECEPTIONIST: Can I have your name, please?

PATIENT: David Cantor.

RECEPTIONIST: Can I see your insurance card?

PATIENT: Here you are.

RECEPTIONIST: OK. You're all set.
Take the elevators to the third floor.
Dr. Mitchell's office is Room 301.

5. Can you recommend a good pediatrician?

▶ *Work in a group.* ▶ *Ask and answer the questions.*

1. What doctors do you see?
2. Can you recommend a good general practitioner? Ophthalmologist? Allergist? Pediatrician?

Use your English!

▶ *With your conversation partner, find out where a medical building is in your community.* ▶ *Report to the class.*

Lesson 5   Going to the Dentist

1. At the dentist's office

🎧 ▸ *Match the numbers and the words.* ▸ *Then listen and repeat.* ▸ *Add words.*

_____ a. braces	_____ e. dentist	_____ i. teeth
_____ b. cavity	_____ f. filling	_____ j. tongue
_____ c. cleaning the	_____ g. giving an anesthetic	k. _____
patient's teeth	_____ h. gums	l. _____
_____ d. dental hygienist		

2. What's happening?

▸ *Answer the questions with your class.*

1. What is the dental hygienist doing?
2. What is the dentist doing?
3. Are the patients afraid?
4. Are they comfortable?

     * Answers are on p. 182.

3. How do you like your dentist?

▶ *Work with a partner. Ask and answer the questions.*

1. When do you go to the dentist? Do you like your dentist?
2. Did you ever have a toothache? What happened?
3. Did the dentist give you an anesthetic?
4. Did you ever wear braces?
5. How often do people in your country visit a dentist?

4. Cross-cultural exchange

▶ *Read the story.* ▶ *Work in a group.* ▶ *Ask and answer the questions.* ▶ *Report to the class.*

| **My tooth fell out.** | **The tooth fairy will come tonight.** | **She'll take my tooth and leave money.** |

1. Do children in your culture believe in the tooth fairy?
2. Does your culture have a different belief about baby teeth? If yes, what is it?

5. Conversation Chant: I Like My Dentist.

🎧 ▶ *Listen.* ▶ *Listen and repeat.* ▶ *Chant with your class.*

I like my dentist.

    She's very nice.

I always follow her advice.

    Do what your dentist tells you to do.

Be nice to your teeth and

they'll be nice to you.

Brush your teeth carefully.

See your dentist frequently.

    Listen to your dentist.

Follow his or her advice.

    Losing a tooth is not very nice.

Use your English!

▶ *Ask your conversation partner: Is there a dentist in your neighborhood? What is the dentist's name? When is the office open?* ▶ *Report to the class.*

Lesson 6   The Hospital

1. At the hospital

🎧 ▶ *Match the numbers and the words.** ▶ *Then listen and repeat.* ▶ *Add words.*

_____ a. aide	_____ f. intravenous	k. _____
_____ b. double room	_____ g. nurse's station	l. _____
_____ c. heart monitor	_____ h. private room	m. _____
_____ d. hospital bed	_____ i. stethoscope	
_____ e. information desk	_____ j. visiting hours	

2. What's in the picture?

▶ *Answer the questions with your class.*

1. What is wrong with the patients?

2. What are the nurses doing?

3. What is the aide doing?

4. Who is the doctor in the picture?

5. Who is very sick?

6. What is the doctor doing with the patient?

3. Visiting hours

🎧 ▶ *Listen and repeat.* ▶ *Practice with a partner.*

RECEPTIONIST: May I help you?

VISITOR: Yes. We're here to visit Betty Master.

RECEPTIONIST: OK. Let me see. She's in room 208.

VISITOR: Thank you.

4. Role play

▶ *Work with a partner.* ▶ *Complete the conversation.* ▶ *Present your role play to the class.*

RECEPTIONIST: May I help you?

VISITOR: _____

RECEPTIONIST: _____

VISITOR: _____

5. Hospital signs

▶ *Work with a partner.* ▶ *Complete the conversations.* ▶ *Compare notes with another pair.*

1. A: I'd like to buy a gift for a patient.
   B: Follow the _____ sign.

2. A: Where can I wait for my friend?
   B: Follow the _____ sign.

3. A: Where can I get some lunch?
   B: Follow the _____ sign.

4. A: How do I get to the 10th floor?
   B: Follow the _____ sign.

5. A: I need to see a doctor right now! I just cut my hand!
   B: Follow the _____ sign.

6. A: Where do I check in?
   B: Admitting or outpatient?
   A: I'm not sure.
   B: Are you staying in the hospital?
   A: Yes.
   B: OK. Follow the _____ sign.

Use your English!

▶ *Ask your conversation partner:* **What hospitals are close to where you live? Have you been to any hospitals? Where? When?** ▶ *Report to the class.*

LISTENING PRACTICE

1. How are you doing?

🎧 ▶ *Listen.* ▶ *Circle a or b.* *

1. What's the matter?
   a. He has a headache.
   b. He has a backache.

2. What does she recommend?
   a. Aspirin.
   b. Cold medicine.

2. Making an appointment

🎧 ▶ *Listen to the conversations.* ▶ *Complete the information in the appointment book.* *

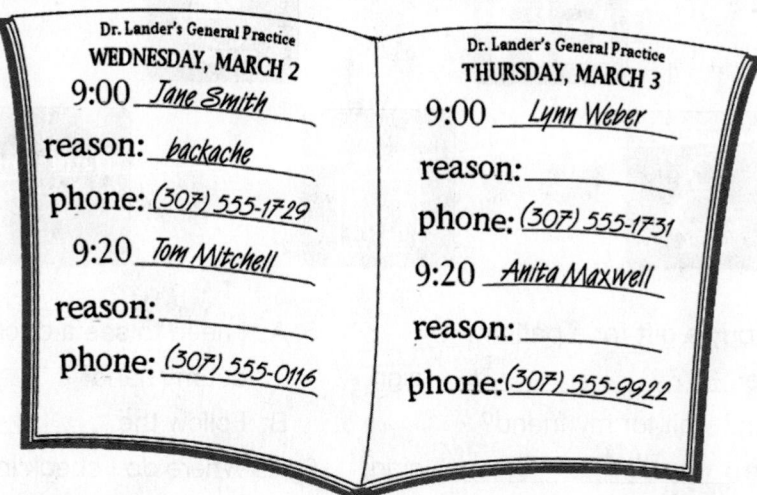

Dr. Lander's General Practice
WEDNESDAY, MARCH 2
9:00 _Jane Smith_
reason: _backache_
phone: _(307) 555-1729_
9:20 _Tom Mitchell_
reason: _____
phone: _(307) 555-0116_

Dr. Lander's General Practice
THURSDAY, MARCH 3
9:00 _Lynn Weber_
reason: _____
phone: _(307) 555-1731_
9:20 _Anita Maxwell_
reason: _____
phone: _(307) 555-9922_

3. Follow the signs!

🎧 ▶ *Listen to the conversations.* ▶ *Write the correct number.*

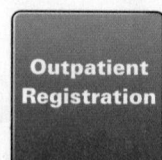

* Answers are on p. 182.

REVIEW

1. Staying healthy

▶ *Answer this question with your class:* **What are some healthy habits?** ▶ *Make a list on the board.*

2. Medicine

▶ *Work in a group of three.* ▶ *Fill in the chart.* ▶ *Report to the class.*

WHAT MEDICINE DO YOU RECOMMEND FOR A. . .	YOU	CLASSMATE 1	CLASSMATE 2
headache?			
stomachache?			
stiff neck?			
cough?			
cold?			
sore throat?			

3. Make a list!

▶ *Work in a group.* ▶ *List words for each subject.* ▶ *Report to the class.*

1. Parts of the body
2. Illnesses
3. Medicines

4. At the doctor's office

▶ *Work with a partner.* ▶ *Complete the conversation between a patient and a receptionist.*

▶ *Present your role play for the class.*

PATIENT: I'm here to see Dr. Banner.

RECEPTIONIST: _____ ?

PATIENT: 3:10.

RECEPTIONIST: _____ ?

PATIENT: I have a stomachache.

RECEPTIONIST: _____ ?

PATIENT: Jim Sanders.

RECEPTIONIST: _____ ?

PATIENT: Certainly. Here it is.

ASSESSMENT

PART 1: Questions

▶ *Write questions to ask a classmate.*

1. Staying healthy: _____

2. Getting sick: _____

3. The pharmacy: _____

4. Doctor visits: _____

5. The dentist: _____

6. The hospital: _____

PART 2: Speaking

▶ *Work with a partner.* ▶ *Ask and answer your questions from Part 1.*

PART 3: Listening

🎧 ▶ *Listen.* ▶ *Circle a or b.* *

1. a. I have a terrible backache.
   b. Here you are.

2. a. From 10:00 to 4:00.
   b. 1:40.

3. a. You should see your dentist!
   b. You should see your obstetrician!

4. a. I have a fever and a sore throat.
   b. Not so well.

5. a. It's Room 201 on the second floor.
   b. Take the elevators.

6. a. From 9:00 to 4:00.
   b. 3:10.

7. a. Sunscreen.
   b. Aspirin.

8. a. I'm sorry to hear that.
   b. I'm glad to hear that.

9. a. Eat well, exercise, and sleep enough.
   b. Give a urine sample, get a blood test, and get a shot.

10. a. Yes. Here you are.
    b. You're all set.

PART 4: Writing

▶ *Write a conversation for this picture.*

RECEPTIONIST: Hello. Dr. Barry's office.

PATIENT: _____

RECEPTIONIST: _____

PATIENT: _____

RECEPTIONIST: _____

PATIENT: _____

* Answers are on p. 182.

UNIT 9
YOUR WORK

PREVIEW

Preview Questions

▶ *Read the questions.* ▶ *What can you answer?*

1. What job do the people in this picture have?
2. What are the workers wearing?
3. What are they doing?

Conversation Tip

▶ *Read the Conversation Tip.* ▶ *Practice with a partner.*

Ask for clarification if you don't understand something.

A: Can you work second shift?
B: I'm sorry. Second shift? **Could you explain that?**
A: Of course. Second shift is from 3:00 P.M. to 11:00 P.M.

Conversation Chant: A Bad Interview

🎧 ▶ *Listen.* ▶ *Listen and repeat.* ▶ *Chant with your class.*

He's talking and she's listening.

    Now she's talking and he's listening.

Now he's talking, but she's not listening.

    Uh-oh!   It's a bad interview!

He's talking, but she's not listening.

    She's talking, but he's not listening.

They're both talking, but nobody's listening.

    Uh-oh!   It's a bad interview!

Lesson 1 Workers and Their Work

① manicurist
② carpenter
③ teacher
④ auto mechanic
⑤ farm worker
⑥ nurse
⑦ barber
⑧ security guard
⑨ TV reporter
⑩ fisherman
⑪ mail carrier
⑫ packer

1. What do they do at work?

🎧 ▸ *Match the workers and their jobs.** ▸ Then listen and repeat.*

_____ a. build with wood	_____ e. drive a tractor	_____ i. repair cars
_____ b. catch fish	_____ f. give manicures	_____ j. report the news
_____ c. cut hair	_____ g. guard a building	_____ k. take care of sick people
_____ d. deliver mail	_____ h. pack boxes	_____ l. teach math

2. Jobs

▸ *Answer the questions with your class.*

1. What are these people's jobs?
2. What do they do?

3. Interesting jobs

▸ *Work in a group.* ▸ *Ask and answer the questions.* ▸ *Tell the class about one of your partners.*

1. Which of these jobs are interesting to you? Which are not?
2. What other jobs are interesting to you?

* Answers are on p. 182.

4. What are they saying?

🎧 ▶ *Listen and repeat.* ▶ *Practice with a partner.*

NANCY: You give great manicures, Angela. Do you like your job?

ANGELA: I love it. How about you, Nancy? What do you do?

NANCY: I'm a bank teller.

ANGELA: What do you do at work?

NANCY: I cash checks and deposit money for customers.

ANGELA: Do you like it?

NANCY: Yes, I do.

5. How about you?

▶ *Work with a partner.* ▶ *Ask and answer the questions.*

1. What's your job?

2. What do you do at work?

3. Do you like your job?

6. The future

▶ *Work in a group.* ▶ *Ask and answer:* **What job would you like to have in the future?**

▶ *Complete the chart.* ▶ *Report to the class.*

NAME	JOB
1. _____	_____
2. _____	_____
3. _____	_____
4. _____	_____

7. Guess who!

▶ *Write your job (or a job you'd like to have) on a piece of paper.* ▶ *Fold the paper.*

▶ *Make a pile.* ▶ *Open one.* ▶ *Read.* ▶ *Guess who it is.*

Use your English!

▶ *Ask your conversation partner:* **What do you do? Do you like your job? What do you do at work? What job would you like to have in the future?**

Lesson 2 Life at Work

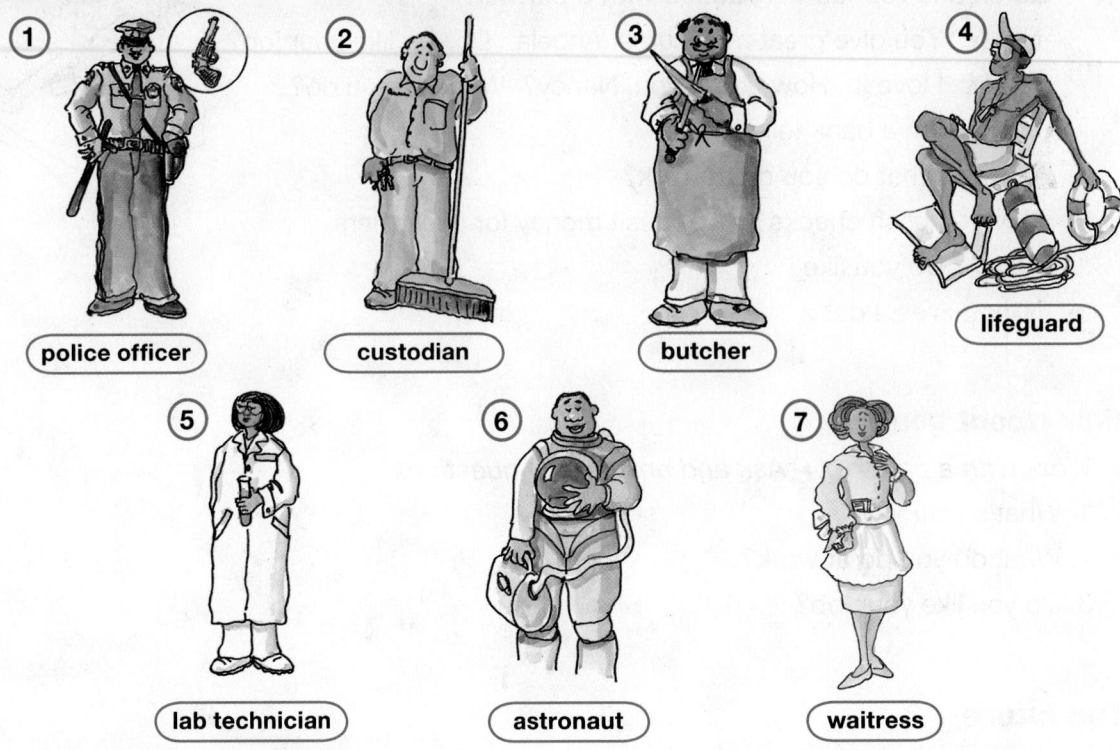

① **police officer** ② **custodian** ③ **butcher** ④ **lifeguard**

⑤ **lab technician** ⑥ **astronaut** ⑦ **waitress**

1. Work clothes and equipment

🎧 ▸ *Match the workers and their clothing or equipment.* ▸ *Use some numbers more than once.**
▸ *Then listen and repeat.* ▸ *Work with a partner.* ▸ *Add words.*

_____ a. apron	_____ f. keys	_____ k. test tube
_____ b. broom	_____ g. lab coat	_____ l. uniform
_____ c. butcher knife	_____ h. life preserver	m. _____
_____ d. gun	_____ i. night stick	n. _____
_____ e. helmet	_____ j. spacesuit	

2. What do they wear at work?

▸ *Answer the questions with your class.*

1. What do the people in the pictures wear at work?

2. What equipment do the they use?

3. What other jobs require uniforms?

3. How about you?

▸ *Work in a group.* ▸ *Ask and answer the questions.* ▸ *Report to the class.*

1. What do you wear at work?

2. What equipment or tools do you use at work? Who pays for the equipment or tools?

                    * Answers are on p. 182.

4. Day job or night job?

🎧 ▶ *Listen and repeat.* ▶ *With a partner fill in the clocks for a day or a night job.* ▶ *Tell the class about Rick.*

1 Rick drives to work.

2 He clocks in.

3 He works as a machinist.

4 He studies on break.

5 He gets a paycheck.

6 He studies at the laundromat.

7 He raises his hand in class.

8 He studies at home.

5. How about you?

▶ *Work with a partner.* ▶ *Ask and answer the questions.*

1. What hours do you work?

2. Do you drive to work?

3. Do you practice English at work?

4. Why are you studying English?

---

6. Conversation Chant: A Day Job or a Night Job?

🎧 ▶ *Listen.* ▶ *Listen and repeat.* ▶ *Chant with your class.*

I'm looking for a day job.

I want to work at night.

I want to see the moon.

I like the morning light.

I like to see the stars.

I love the Milky Way.

I want to see the sun come up .

I like a sunny day .

I'm looking for a day job.

I want to work at night.

I love the darkness.

I love the light.

Use your English!

▶ *With your conversation partner, list jobs in your community that require uniforms.* ▶ *Report to the class.*

Lesson 3 Looking for a Job

HELP WANTED

✚ Nurses Wanted ✚

f/t + p/t, RN + LPN, for home health care visits.
Salary DOE.
Bilingual pref., refs. reqd.
Must have own transportation.
Call (978) 336-4202.

CARPENTER

Wanted: Experienced carpenter.
Steady work. Must have own transportation. Pay DOE.
Call 249-8064.

Packer

No exp. req'd. We train.
Openings, 1st, 2nd, and 3rd shfts.
$7/hr.
Apply in person at Hot Chili Canning Co., 4470 Hatch Highway.

Math Teacher

Grades 7-8 in excellent new elementary school. Teaching exp. and refs. req'd.
Bilingual pref., salary DOE.
Send resume to P.O. Box 7716, Eagle View, CA 91925

Security Guard

P/t and f/t, 3rd shft. Drug test and refs.req'd. Exp. pref. Pay DOE.
Apply in person at Security Office, West Side Mall, Speedway Blvd.

1. Help wanted ads

🎧 ▸ *Match the abbreviations with their full words.* * ▸ *Listen and repeat.* ▸ *Read the newspaper ads with your class.*

WORDS	ABBREVIATIONS
_____ 1. company	a. 1st shft.
_____ 2. first shift (7:00 A.M.–3:00 P.M.)	b. 2nd shft.
_____ 3. full-time	c. 3rd shft.
_____ 4. Registered Nurse	d. Co.
_____ 5. references required	e. DOE
_____ 6. depends on experience	f. exp. req'd.
_____ 7. second shift (3:00P.M.–11:00 P.M.)	g. f/t
_____ 8. preferred	h. LPN
_____ 9. part-time	i. p/t
_____ 10. third shift (11:00 P.M.–7:00 A.M.)	j. pref.
_____ 11. experience required	k. RN
_____ 12. Licensed Practical Nurse	l. refs. req'd.

* Answers are on p. 182.

2. What do the ads mean?

▶ *Work with a group.* ▶ *Answer the questions.* ▶ *Ask:* **Could you explain that?**
▶ *Report to the class.*

1. Which jobs require references? Experience? Your own transportation?
2. Which ads say "apply in person"? Which ads have a telephone number to call?
3. Which jobs are full-time? Part-time? Which ads don't say?
4. In which jobs does pay depend on experience?
5. Which jobs are for the first shift? The second shift? The third shift? Which ads don't say?
6. Which ads say "bilingual preferred"? What other jobs prefer bilingual workers?

3. Help wanted in your community

▶ *Work in a group.* ▶ *Tell your group about any job openings in your community.*
▶ *Make a list of job openings.* ▶ *Report to the class.*

4. Replying to a help wanted ad

▶ *Work with a partner.* ▶ *Complete the phone conversation.* ▶ *Present your role play to the class.*

EMPLOYER: May I help you?

APPLICANT: Yes. My name is _____ . I'm calling about your ad in the
paper for a _____ .

EMPLOYER: Yes, we're looking for a _____ . Can you come in and fill out an
application?

APPLICANT: I can come this afternoon.

EMPLOYER: Fine. The address is _____ .

APPLICANT: Thank you. I'll see you this afternoon.

Use your English!

▶ *With your conversation partner, look in a local newspaper or on the
Internet for jobs.* ▶ *Find several opportunities.* ▶ *Report the information
to the class.*

P

PORTER HOSPITAL

APPLICATION FOR EMPLOYMENT

DATE: February 20, 2008
               (Month) (Day) (Year)

NAME: Carmen   A.   Mendoza
           (First)   (Middle Initial)   (Last)

ADDRESS: 25   Marshall Rd.
           (Number)   (Street)   (Apartment Number)
           Greenville, Kentucky   42158
           (City)   (State)   (Zip Code)

TELEPHONE: (734) 621-4908
           (Area Code)

JOB YOU'RE APPLYING FOR: Nurse (Surgical)

WORK EXPERIENCE:

Surgical Nurse, Porter Hospital, Greenville, 1999-2004

(Job)	(Employer)	(Address)	(Date)
(Job)	(Employer)	(Address)	(Date)

EDUCATION:

Parks College	R.N.	1998
(School/College)	(Degree/Diploma/Certificate)	(Date)
Greenville H.S.	Diploma	1993
(School/College)	(Degree/Diploma/Certificate)	(Date)

REFERENCES:

Janet Wong	Nursing Head Porter Hospital	(734)553-0801
(Name)	(Position)	(Phone Number)
Donna Hunt	Nurse, Porter Hospital	(734)582-82-44
(Name)	(Position)	(Phone Number)

---

1. Carmen's application

▶ *Read Carmen's application with your class.* ▶ *Answer the questions.* *

1. Where does Carmen live?
2. What's her phone number?
3. What job is she applying for?
4. What experience does she have?
5. What education does she have?
6. Who are her references?

2. Carmen's job interview

▶ *Work with a partner.* ▶ *Write three questions for the job interviewer and three questions for Carmen.* ▶ *Role-play Carmen's job interview, using her application.*

JOB INTERVIEWER'S QUESTIONS	CARMEN'S QUESTIONS

3. Your job application

▶ *Fill out the job application for yourself.* ▶ *Work with a partner.* ▶ *Read each other's job applications.*

APPLICATION FOR EMPLOYMENT

DATE: _____
(Month) (Day) (Year)

NAME: _____
(First)   (Middle Initial)   (Last)

ADDRESS: _____
(Number)   (Street)   (Apartment Number)

_____
(City)   (State)   (Zip Code)

TELEPHONE: ( )_____
(Area Code)

JOB YOU'RE APPLYING FOR: _____

WORK EXPERIENCE:

_____
(Job)   (Employer)   (Address)   (Date)

_____
(Job)   (Employer)   (Address)   (Date)

EDUCATION:

_____
(School/College)   (Degree/Diploma/Certificate)   (Date)

_____
(School/College)   (Degree/Diploma/Certificate)   (Date)

REFERENCES:

_____
(Name)   (Position)   (Phone Number)

_____
(Name)   (Position)   (Phone Number)

4. Your job interview role play

▶ *Work with a partner.* ▶ *Use your job applications.* ▶ *Interview your partner for a job.*

▶ *Ask:* **Could you explain that?**

Use your English!

▶ *With your conversation partner, get job-application forms in your community.*

▶ *With your class, compare the application forms.* ▶ *What information is on all the forms?*

Lesson 5 Safety at Work

1. Safety clothing, signs, and equipment

🎧 ▶ *Match the numbers and the sentences.* * ▶ *Then listen and repeat.* ▶ *Add words.*

_____ a. broken leg	_____ e. heavy shirt	_____ i. STOP sign
_____ b. face shield	_____ f. NO SMOKING sign	_____ j. welding gloves
_____ c. fall	_____ g. road repair crew	k. _____
_____ d. hard hat	_____ h. safety cone	l. _____

2. Safety on the job

▶ *Answer these questions with your class.*

1. What safety signs are in the pictures? What do they mean?

2. What safety clothing is the welder wearing? What are the construction workers wearing?

3. What safety equipment are they using?

4. What other jobs require safety clothing, equipment or signs?

5. What other safety signs do you see every day?

7. Why do you think the woman fell? What happened to her?

3. Cross-cultural exchange

▶ *Answer the questions with your class.*

1. What safety clothing do people wear in your country?

2. What safety signs are there in your country?

3. In your country what jobs require asbestos gloves? Hard hats?

4. In your country where are there NO SMOKING signs? STOP signs? Safety cones?

* Answers are on p. 183.

4. Safety violations

🎧 ▶ *Listen and repeat.* ▶ *Practice with a partner.* ▶ *Answer the questions with your class.*

LAB TECHNICIAN: No! Don't come in!

WORKER: Why not? What's the matter?

LAB TECHNICIAN: Look at the sign! It says "No Admittance!" This is a "clean" room. You can't come in!

WORKER: Oh, sorry. I'll leave now.

1. What do employees have to wear in the "clean" room?
2. What does the sign say on the door?
3. What other safety violations do you see in the picture?
4. Who is clocking out? Where is he going?

5. Role play

▶ *Work in a group.* ▶ *Complete the conversation.* ▶ *Present your role play to the class.*

WORKER 1: Ha-ha-ha. That's great!

WORKER 2: _____

SUPERVISOR: _____

Use your English!

▶ *With your conversation partner, make a list of safety signs in your community.*

▶ *Report to your class.*

Lesson 6 Leaving a Job

1. Layoffs

🎧 ▸ *Match the numbers and the sentences.* ▸ *Use some numbers more than once.**

▸ *Then listen and repeat.*

_____ a. Business is bad.

_____ b. Business is good.

_____ c. The last worker is laid off.

_____ d. Pete's Pickles has many workers.

_____ e. Pete's Pickles has only one worker.

_____ f. Pete's Pickles is closed.

2. How's business in your city?

▸ *Answer the questions with your class.*

1. Is business good or bad now in your city?

2. Are any companies hiring new employees?

3. Are any companies laying off employees?

4. Does anyone in your class have experience with layoffs?

3. You're fired!

▸ *With a partner, answer the questions.* ▸ *Report to the class.*

1. What's Henry doing?

2. What's his job?

3. Why does the boss fire Henry?

4. What are good reasons to fire an employee?

* Answers are on p. 183.

4. Leaving a job

🎧 ▶ *Match the numbers and the words.* * ▶ *Then listen and repeat.*

_____ a. baby shower

_____ b. Congratulations!

_____ c. getting a promotion

_____ d. good luck!

_____ e. having a baby

_____ f. moving away

5. Good reasons to leave a job

▶ *Answer the questions with your class.*

1. Why are these people leaving or changing their jobs?

2. What's happening in the pictures?

3. What are other good reasons to leave a job?

---

6. Conversation Chant: Out of Work

🎧 ▶ *Listen.* ▶ *Listen and repeat.* ▶ *Chant with your class.*

What's the matter?

    I just spoke to Ray.

    He got laid off yesterday.

Bob lost his job.

    So did Sue.

Fred got fired.

    Mack did, too.

What about Fay?

    She's OK, but they asked her to take

    some leave without pay.

Use your English!

▶ *Ask your conversation partner:* **What are good reasons to leave a job?**

What are good reasons for a boss to fire an employee?

LISTENING PRACTICE

1. I'm calling about the job.

🎧 ▶ *Listen.* ▶ *Circle a or b.* *

1. Where did Jim see the want ad?
   a. On the Internet.
   b. In the newspaper.
2. What is the company looking for?
   a. A carpenter.
   b. A driver.
3. What does an applicant have to have?
   a. A high school diploma.
   b. A car.

4. When is Jim's appointment?
   a. Today.
   b. Tomorrow.
5. What time is his appointment?
   a. 4:00.
   b. 5:00.

2. What do you do?

🎧 ▶ *Listen.* ▶ *Circle a or b.*

1. What does Annie do?
   a. She's a firefighter.
   b. She's a teacher.
2. What's Michael's job?
   a. He's a police officer.
   b. He's a security guard.
3. Whose job is new?
   a. Annie's
   b. Michael's

4. Why does Michael like his job?
   a. It's quiet.
   b. He likes dangerous work.
5. Does Annie like her job?
   a. Yes, she does.
   b. No, she doesn't.

3. Questions and answers

🎧 ▶ *Listen.* ▶ *Circle a or b.* *

1. a. I'm a security guard.
   b. Yes, I have a good job.
2. a. I'm a nurse.
   b. Work as an auto mechanic.
3. a. The company.
   b. Employees have to wear a uniform at work.
4. a. I work from 8:00 A.M. to 4:30 P.M.
   b. I work Monday to Friday.

5. a. She got a promotion.
   b. She was fired.
6. a. I love it. I like working at night.
   b. I don't like it very much. I'm really a night owl.
7. a. Yes, from 2:00 to 4:00 Mondays and Fridays.
   b. No, my job is only part time.
8. a. Business at the restaurant was very bad.
   b. He was late for work every day for a month.

* Answers are on p. 183.

REVIEW

1. **Make a list!**

    ▶ *Work with a partner.* ▶ *How many jobs can you think of in five minutes?* ▶ *Make a list.*

    ▶ *Compare lists with two other pairs.* ▶ *Who had the most jobs?*

2. **At work**

    ▶ *Work with a partner.* ▶ *Ask and answer the questions.*

    1. What do you wear at work?
    2. What hours do you work?
    3. What do you do at work?
    4. What day is payday?
    5. Do you like your job?

3. **Help wanted ads**

    ▶ *Work with a partner.* ▶ *Decide on an interesting job.* ▶ *Write a Help Wanted ad for the job.*

    ▶ *Read your ad to the class.*

4. **Applying for a job**

    ▶ *Work with a partner.* ▶ *Write a phone conversation about a Help Wanted ad.* ▶ *Present your conversation to the class.*

5. **Safety at work**

    ▶ *Work in a group.* ▶ *Make a list of three safety signs at work, three kinds of safety clothing for work, and three safety rules at work.* ▶ *Share your ideas with another group or with the class.*

6. **Leaving a job**

    ▶ *Ask four students:* **What's a good reason to leave a job?**

ASSESSMENT

PART 1: Questions

▶ *Write questions to ask a classmate.*

1. Your job: _____

2. Work clothing: _____

3. Looking for a job: _____

4. Work experience: _____

5. Safety at work: _____

6. Leaving a job: _____

PART 2: Speaking

▶ *Work with a partner.* ▶ *Ask and answer your questions from Part 1.*

PART 3: Listening

🎧 ▶ *Listen.* ▶ *Circle a or b.**

1. a. I'm getting a promotion.

   b. Yes, I am.

2. a. Yes, I love it.

   b. No, I'm not.

3. a. Because I don't like working as a teller.

   b. Because I have experience as a teller.

4. a. I was a farm worker.

   b. I worked in Los Angeles.

5. a. Yes, I do.

   b. I like the work, and the pay is good.

PART 4: Writing

▶ *Write a conversation for this picture.*

Boss: _____

Henry: _____

Boss: _____

* Answers are on p. 183.

UNIT 10
YOUR FREE TIME

PREVIEW

Preview Questions

▶ *Read the questions.* ▶ *What can you answer?*

1. Where are the people in the picture?
2. What are they doing?
3. What day of the week do you think it is?
   Explain your answer.

Conversation Tip

▶ *Read the Conversation Tip.* ▶ *Practice with a partner.*

Express agreement and disagreement about what you like.

A: I like to go to the park on Saturdays.
B: **So do I!** And I like to jog at the park.
A: **Oh, I don't!** I don't like to jog at all.

A: I don't like horror movies.
B: **Neither do I.** Do you like comedies?
A: Yes, I do.
B: **I do, too.**

Conversation Chant: I Love to Fly

🎧 ▶ *Listen.* ▶ *Listen and repeat.* ▶ *Chant with your class.*

I love to fly.

    So do I.

I don't like the bus.

    Neither do I.

I'm always in a hurry.

    So am I.

I guess that's why

I love to fly.

I love the mountains,

And I love to ski.

I'm a sailor

I love the sea.

Lesson 1 Going Out

1. People and places

🎧 ▶ *Match the numbers and the words.** ▶ Then listen and repeat.* ▶ *Add words.*

Places to go to . . .	_____ e. the movies	**People to go with . . .**
_____ a. an amusement park	_____ f. a nightclub	_____ j. children
_____ b. an art museum	_____ g. a party	_____ k. a date
_____ c. the ballpark	_____ h. the theater	_____ l. friends
_____ d. a concert	i. _____	m. _____

* Answers are on p. 183.

2. Good places to go

▶ *Answer the questions with your class.*

1. What's the name of a museum in your town? A nightclub? An amusement park? A theater? A ballpark? A movie theater? A concert hall?

2. What's a good place to take children?

3. What's a good place to take a tourist?

4. What's a good place to take your family?

3. How about you?

▶ *Work with a group.* ▶ *Answer the questions.*

1. Where do you like to go when you go out?

2. What places do you recommend?

4. Invitations

🎧 ▶ *Listen and repeat.* ▶ *Practice with a partner.*

CONVERSATION 1

GEORGE: Would you like to go to the movies with me on Saturday?

MARY: Sure! I'd love to! What do you want to see?

GEORGE: *Mystery on the Lake.*

MARY: That sounds great. What time?

GEORGE: There are shows at 7:00 and 9:00.

MARY: How about the 7:00 show?

GEORGE: OK.

CONVERSATION 2

TOM: Would you like to go to a concert with me on Saturday?

MARY: Oh, I'm sorry. I already have plans.

TOM: That's OK. Maybe some other time.

MARY: Sure.

5. Role play

▶ *Work with a partner.* ▶ *Write a conversation.* ▶ *Invite someone to do something.*

▶ *Present your conversation to the class.*

Use your English!

▶ *With your conversation partner, make a list of interesting places in your city or town to take a visitor.* ▶ *Report to the class.*

Lesson 2 Free Time

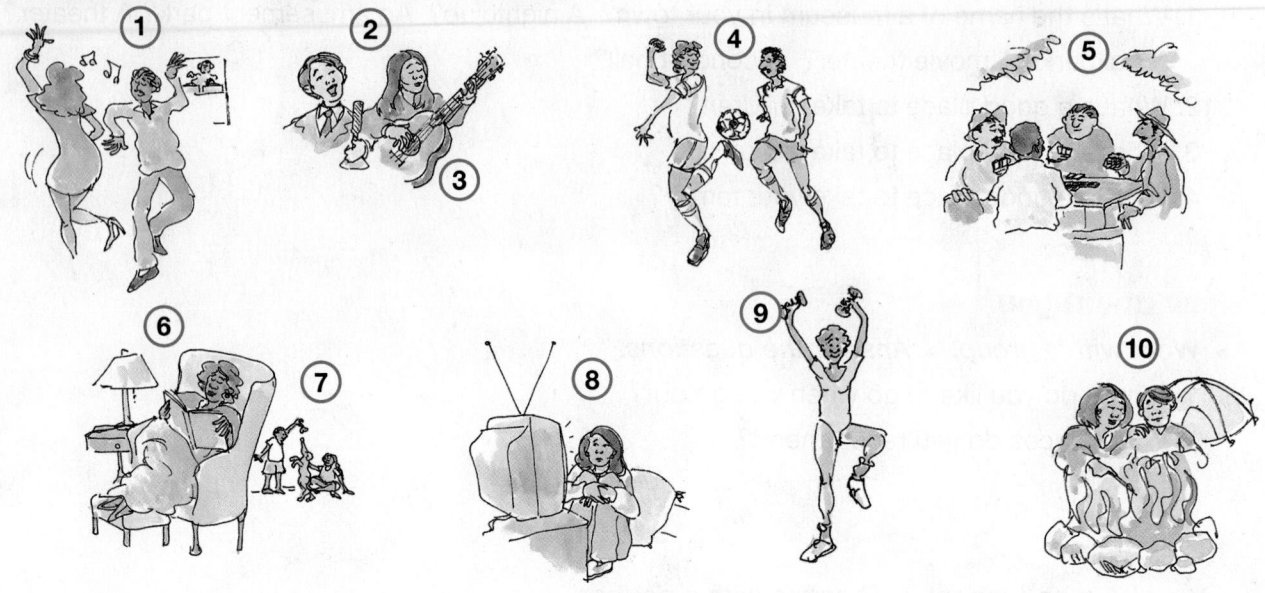

1. Free-time activities

🎧 ▶ *Match the numbers and the words.** ▶ Then listen and repeat. ▶ Add other free-time activities.*

_____ a. dance		_____ e. play dominoes		_____ i. sing	
_____ b. exercise with weights		_____ f. play the guitar		_____ j. watch TV	
_____ c. go camping		_____ g. play soccer		k. _____	
_____ d. play with a dog		_____ h. read a book		l. _____	

2. What do they do in their free time?

▶ *Work with a partner.* ▶ *Ask about the people in the pictures:* **What does she do in her free time? What does he do in his free time? What do they do in their free time?**

3. Conversation Chant: Free-time Fun

🎧 ▶ *Listen.* ▶ *Listen and repeat.* ▶ *Chant with your class.*

I love to go camping.

Not me. I don't like camping at all.

I like hot weather.

I don't . I like the spring or the fall.

I never go out without my phone.

I love to go to the movies alone.

I love big parties down by the sea.

Dinner for two sounds great to me.

* Answers are on p. 183.

4. How often . . . ?

▸ *Work in a group.* ▸ *Ask and answer the questions.* ▸ *Count the answers and report to the class.*

HOW OFTEN DO YOU . . .	OFTEN	SOMETIMES	NEVER
1. watch TV?			
2. exercise?			
3. read a book?			
4. dance?			
5. go to the movies?			
6. go to a museum?			
7. go to a party?			
8. go to a concert?			
9. go to an amusement park?			

5. Free time

🎧 ▸ *Listen and repeat.* ▸ *Practice with a partner.*

A: I like to go to parties.
B: So do I! And I love to sing with my friends.
A: Oh, I don't! But I love to dance.

6. How about you?

▸ *Make a list of all the things you like to do in your free time.*
▸ *Work with a partner.*
▸ *Compare your lists.*
▸ *What do you both like to do?*

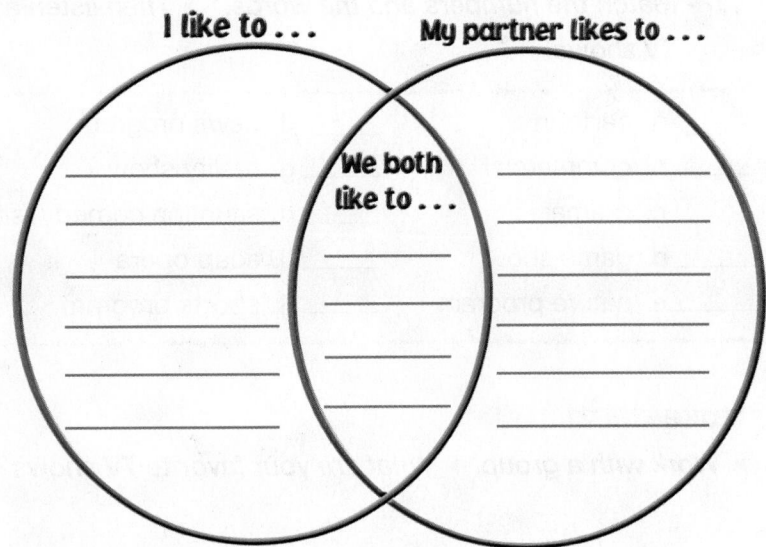

I like to . . .   My partner likes to . . .

We both like to . . .

▸ *With your conversation partner, look in the newspaper or on the Internet.*
▸ *Find out what's happening in your town or city this weekend.* ▸ *Make plans.*
▸ *Report to the class.*

1. TV shows

🎧 ▶ *Match the numbers and the words.** ▶ Then listen and repeat.* ▶ *Add other kinds of TV shows.*

_____ a. cartoon	_____ f. news program	_____ k. talk show
_____ b. commercial	_____ g. reality show	l. _____
_____ c. drama	_____ h. situation comedy (sitcom)	m. _____
_____ d. game show	_____ i. soap opera	n. _____
_____ e. nature program	_____ j. sports program	

2. Make a list!

▶ *Work with a group.* ▶ *What are your favorite TV shows?* ▶ *Make a list.* ▶ *Report to the class.*

3. How about you?

▶ *Work with a partner.* ▶ *Ask and answer the questions.*

1. How much TV do you watch? When do you watch TV?
2. How many TVs do you have in your home?
3. Who watches the most TV in your family?

* Answers are on p. 183.

4. At the video store

🎧 ▶ *Match the numbers and the words.** ▶ *Then listen and repeat.* ▶ *Add words.*

_____ a. action movies

_____ b. comedies

_____ c. dramas

_____ d. family movies

_____ e. horror movies

_____ f. love stories

_____ g. mysteries

_____ h. science-fiction

_____ i. westerns

j. _____

k. _____

l. _____

5. What kinds of movies do you like?

🎧 ▶ *Listen and repeat.* ▶ *Practice with a partner.*

A: What kinds of movies do you like?

B: I like westerns.

A: I don't! I like action movies.

B: Me, too.

6. Find someone who . . .

▶ *Talk to your classmates.* ▶ *Ask the questions.* ▶ *Write names to complete the sentences.*

▶ *Report to the class.*

1.	_____	never watches movies.
2.	_____	doesn't like horror movies.
3.	_____	likes TV reality shows.
4.	_____	watches at least three hours of TV a day.
5.	_____	likes science-fiction movies.
6.	_____	doesn't like love stories.

Use your English!

▶ *Ask your conversation partner:* **What TV shows are popular in your country?**

---

* Answers are on p. 183.

1. At the park

🎧 ▸ *Match the numbers and the words.** ▸ Then listen and repeat.* ▸ *Add words.*

_____ a. feed the birds	_____ e. play Frisbee	i. _____
_____ b. fly a kite	_____ f. play in the playground	j. _____
_____ c. have a picnic	_____ g. ride a bike	k. _____
_____ d. jog	_____ h. take a walk	

2. What's happening?

▸ *Answer the questions with your class.*

1. What are the people doing in the park?

2. What do you think? What day of the week is it? What time of day is it?

3. What do you like to do in the park?

* Answers are on p. 183.

3. Conversation Chant: The Beautiful Park

🎧 ▶ *Listen.* ▶ *Listen and repeat.* ▶ *Chant with your class.*

I love to walk in the park.

Under the trees in the park.

Under the tall, beautiful trees.

I love to walk in the park.

I love to watch the families in the park

Flying kites in the park.

Having picnics, feeding the birds,

playing with their babies in the park.

Tall trees, hungry birds,

Beautiful babies, beautiful park.

Tall trees, hungry babies.

Beautiful babies, beautiful park.

4. What's the story?

▶ *Work with a partner.* ▶ *Answer the questions and make up a story.* ▶ *Tell your story to the class.*

1. What are these people's names?
2. What day of the week is it? What time of the year is it?
3. What are the people doing?
4. How are they feeling?

5. How about you?

▶ *Work with a partner.* ▶ *Ask and answer the questions.*

1. Do you live near a park?
2. What's the name of the park?
3. How often do you go to the park?
4. What day of the week do you usually go to the park? What time?
5. Who do you usually go with?
6. What do you do there?

Use your English!

▶ *Ask your conversation partner:* **What is a popular park in your neigborhood? What do people do there?**

Lesson 5 Sports

1. Individual sports

🎧 ▸ *Match the numbers and words.* * ▸ *Then listen and repeat.* ▸ *Add words.*

_____ a. bowling	_____ f. ice-skating	_____ k. yoga
_____ b. boxing	_____ g. skiing	l. _____
_____ c. golf	_____ h. swimming	m. _____
_____ d. gymnastics	_____ i. tennis	n. _____
_____ e. hiking	_____ j. wrestling	

2. What's the sport?

▸ *Work in a group.* ▸ *Act out a sport.* ▸ *Have the group guess.* ▸ *Then present one pantomime to the class.* ▸ *Have the class guess.*

* Answers are on p. 183.

3. Team sports

🎧 ▶ *Match the numbers and the words.** ▶ Then listen and repeat. ▶ Add names of other team sports.*

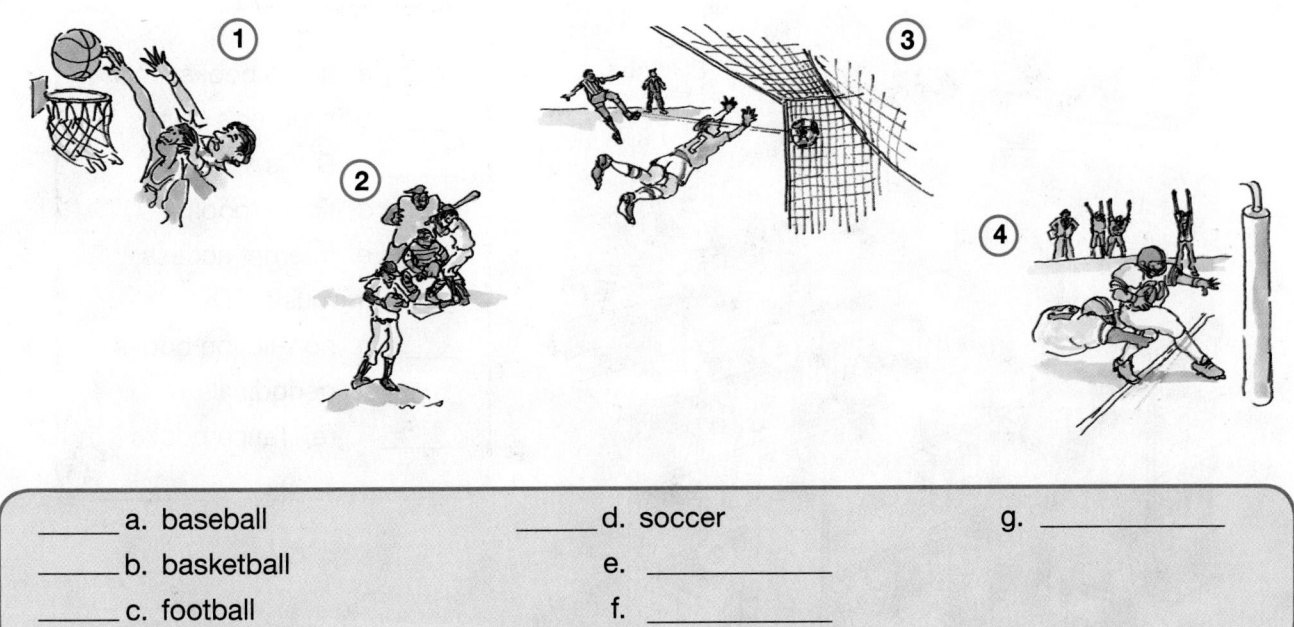

_____	a. baseball	_____	d. soccer	g.	_____
_____	b. basketball	e.	_____		
_____	c. football	f.	_____		

4. Professional teams

▶ *Work in a group.* ▶ *How many teams for each sport can you list?* ▶ *Report to the class.*

5. What's your favorite?

▶ *Write your answers to the questions.* ▶ *Work in a group of three.* ▶ *Ask:* **What's your favorite _____ ?** ▶ *Report the group's answers to the class.*

WHAT'S YOUR FAVORITE . . .	YOU	CLASSMATE 1	CLASSMATE 2
sport to watch?	_____	_____	_____
sports team?	_____	_____	_____
sport to play?	_____	_____	_____

Use your English!

▶ *Ask your conversation partner:* **What team sports are popular in your country? What sports do boys play? What sports do girls play?** ▶ *Report to the class.*

---

* Answers are on p. 183.

Lesson 6 Lifelong Learning

a. audio books

b. children's books

c. DVDs

d. fiction books

e. Internet access

f. music CDs

g. non-fiction books

h. periodicals

i. reference books

1. At the library

🎧 ▸ *Match the numbers with the words.** ▸ *Then listen and repeat.*

2. What can you borrow from the public library?

▸ *Answer the questions with your class.*

1. What can you borrow from the public library?

2. What kinds of books do you like?

3. Do you ever listen to audio books?

3. Find someone who . . .

▸ *Talk to your classmates.* ▸ *Ask the questions.* ▸ *Write names to complete the sentences.*
▸ *Report to the class.*

1. _____	often goes to the library.
2. _____	borrows books from the library.
3. _____	borrows music CDs from the library.
4. _____	never goes to the library.
5. _____	goes to the library with his or her children.

* Answers are on p. 183.

4. Continuing education classes

▶ *Work in a group. Ask and answer the questions.*

1. Does your English school offer classes in other subjects? Which ones?

2. Would you like to take a class in a different subject? What subject? Explain your answer.

3. Would you like to take a class in cake decorating? Why or why not?

5. Your work/education plan

▶ *Work in a group.* ▶ *Talk about your future plans.* ▶ *Ask and answer the questions.*

▶ *Report to the class.*

1. What job do you want to have in five years?

2. What do you need to learn to get that job?

3. Are there classes you need to take?   How much English do you need for the classes? Where can you take the classes? How much do the classes cost?

4. What other ways are there to learn the job?

6. Plans for learning more English

▶ *Work in a group.* ▶ *List ways to learn more English.* ▶ *Report to the class.*

Use your English!

▶ *With your conversation partner, find out which schools offer continuing education classes in your community.* ▶ *Report to the class.*

LISTENING PRACTICE

1. What do they like to do in their free time?

🎧 ▶ *Listen to the conversation.* ▶ *Complete the chart.**

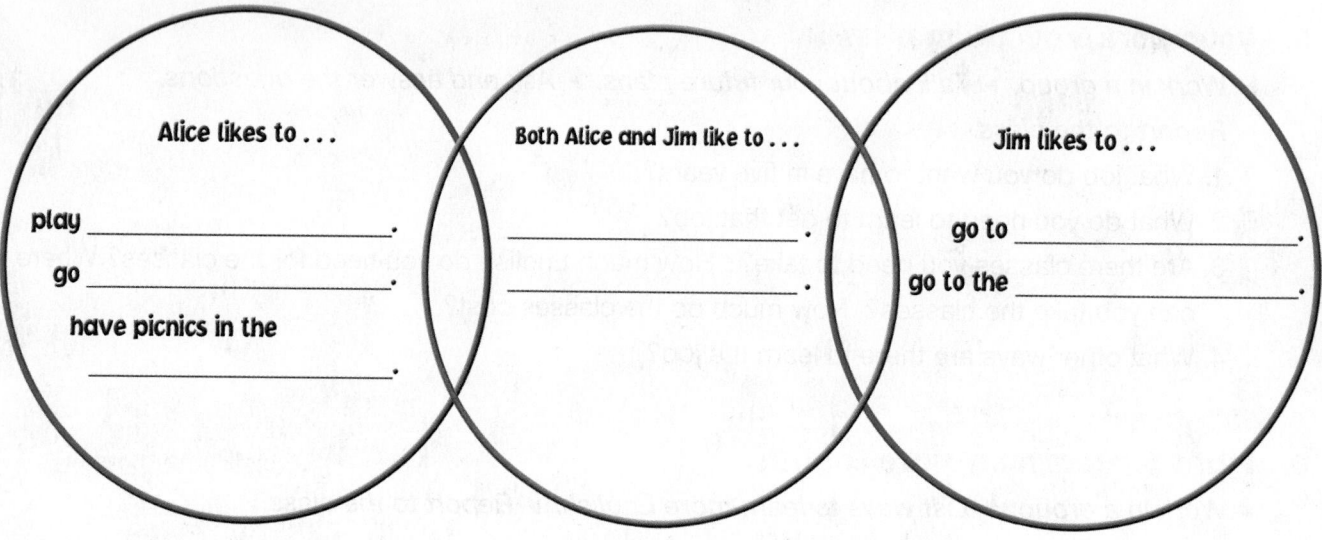

Alice likes to . . .

play _____ .

go _____ .

have picnics in the

_____ .

Both Alice and Jim like to . . .

_____ .

_____ .

Jim likes to . . .

go to _____ .

go to the _____ .

2. Going out

🎧 ▶ *Listen.* ▶ *Circle a or b.**

1. Where are they going?
   a. To a concert.
   b. To a nightclub.

2. When is their date?
   a. Saturday night.
   b. Sunday night.

3. About you

🎧 ▶ *Listen.* ▶ *Write your answers.* ▶ *Work in a group.* ▶ *Read your answers to the group.*

1. _____
2. _____
3. _____
4. _____
5. _____
6. _____
7. _____

* Answers are on p. 183.

REVIEW

1. Who is it?

▶ *Write your answers to the questions on a piece of paper.* ▶ *Fold your paper.* ▶ *Make a pile.*

▶ *Open one.* ▶ *Read.* ▶ *Guess who it is.*

1. What do you like to do in your free time?

2. Where do you like to go when you go out?

3. What are your favorite TV shows?

4. What are your favorite sports?

2. What am I doing?

▶ *Work in a group.* ▶ *Act out a free-time activity.* ▶ *Have the group guess the activity.*

▶ *Then present one pantomime to the class.* ▶ *Have the class guess.*

3. So do I!

▶ *Agree or disagree with Harry's statements.*

1. HARRY: I like to play soccer.

    YOU: _____

2. HARRY: I like to go to amusement parks.

    YOU: _____

3. HARRY: I like to dance.

    YOU: _____

4. HARRY: I don't like to watch nature programs.

    YOU: _____

5. HARRY: I don't like to go to concerts.

    YOU: _____

4. What sports do you like?

▶ *Make a list of all the sports you like.* ▶ *Work with a partner.* ▶ *Compare your lists.* ▶ *What sports do you both like?* ▶ *Report to the class.*

5. Libraries

▶ *Work with a partner.* ▶ *List all the things you can do at a library.* ▶ *Report to the class.*

ASSESSMENT

PART 1: Questions

▶ *Write questions to ask a classmate.*

1. Going out: _____
2. Free time: _____
3. TV and movies: _____
4. At the park: _____
5. Sports: _____
6. Lifelong learning: _____

PART 2: Speaking

▶ *Work with a partner.* ▶ *Ask and answer your questions from Part 1.*

PART 3: Listening

🎧 ▶ *Listen.* ▶ *Circle a or b.**

1. a. No, I don't.
   b. Sure. I'd love to!
2. a. I exercised last Saturday.
   b. I never exercise.
3. a. I like to watch sports programs on TV and go to the movies.
   b. Oh, I don't like it at all!
4. a. Yes, I love to go to the movies.
   b. Action movies and westerns.

5. a. Internet access and reference books.
   b. Books, audio books, movies, and music CDs.
6. a. Football.
   b. Go to parties and play music.
7. a. Never.
   b. 8:00 and 10:00.
8. a. So do I.
   b. Neither do I.

Part 4: Writing

▶ *Write a conversation for this picture.*

WOMAN: What do you like to do in your free time?

MAN: _____

WOMAN: _____

MAN: _____

WOMAN: _____

MAN: _____

* Answers are on p. 183.

Map of the U.S.A. and Canada

Questions

1. Who in your class is from the United States? Which state?
2. Who in your class is from Canada? Which province?
3. What languages do people speak in the United States? In Canada?
4. Who has visited the United States or Canada?

Map of Mexico, Central America, and the Caribbean

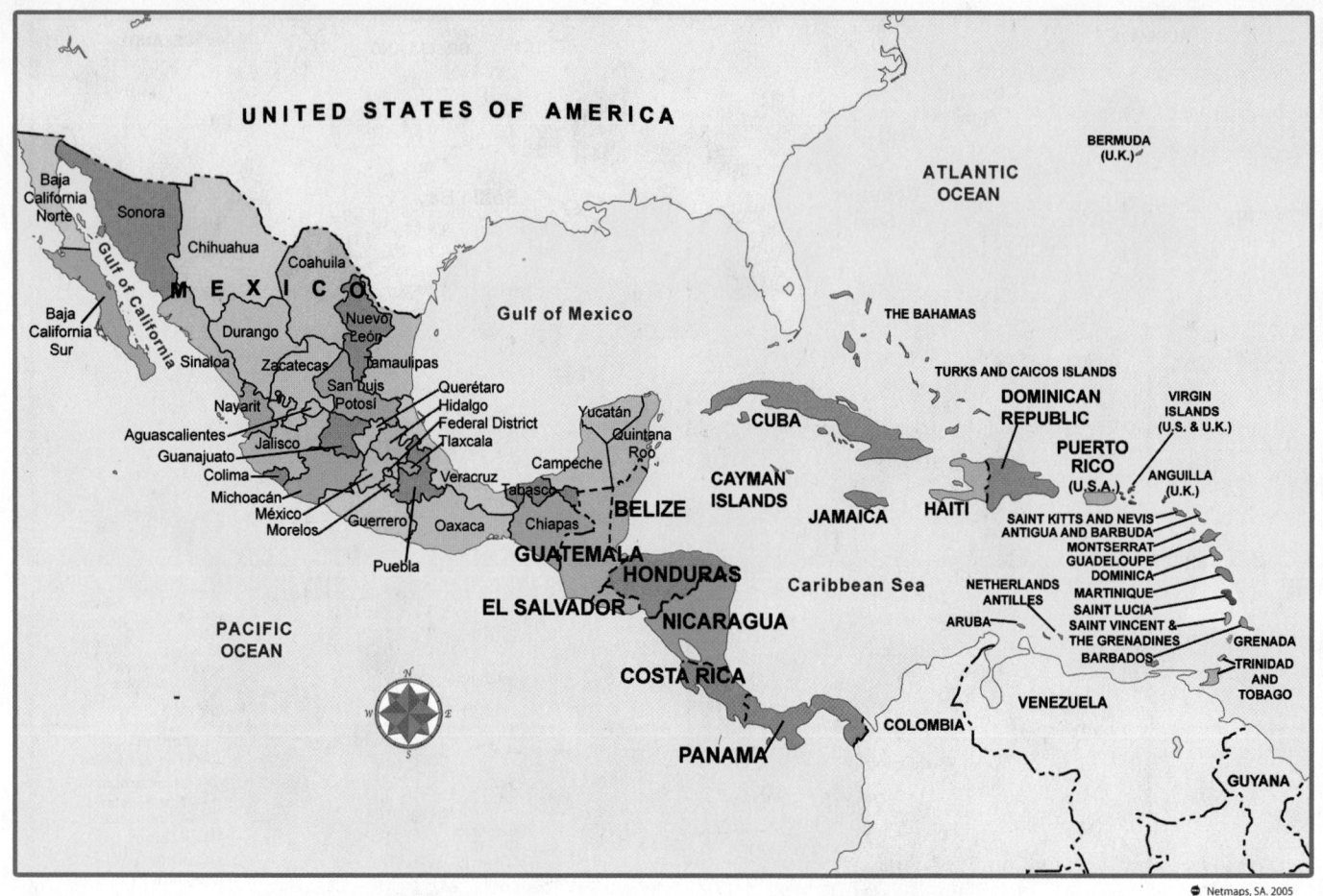

Questions

1. Who in your class is from Mexico? What state? What languages do people speak there?
2. Who is from Central America? What country? What languages do people speak there?
3. Who is from an island in the Caribbean? An island in the Atlantic?
4. What languages do your classmates speak?

Map of South America

NICARAGUA
COSTA RICA
PANAMA
Caribbean
Sea
GRENADA
TRINIDAD AND TOBAGO
VENEZUELA
GUYANA
SURINAME
FRENCH
GUIANA
COLOMBIA
ECUADOR
GALAPAGOS
ISLANDS
PERÚ
BRAZIL
BOLIVIA
PACIFIC
OCEAN
PARAGUAY
CHILE
ATLANTIC
OCEAN
URUGUAY
ARGENTINA
Chiloé Island
Strait of
Magellan
FALKLAND
ISLANDS
(U.K.)
SOUTH GEORGIA
ISLAND
(U.K.)
Santa Inés Island
Tierra del Fuego
Cape Horn

Questions

1. Who in your class is from South America?

2. What country is your classmate from?

3. What languages do people speak in that country?

Map of Asia and Australia

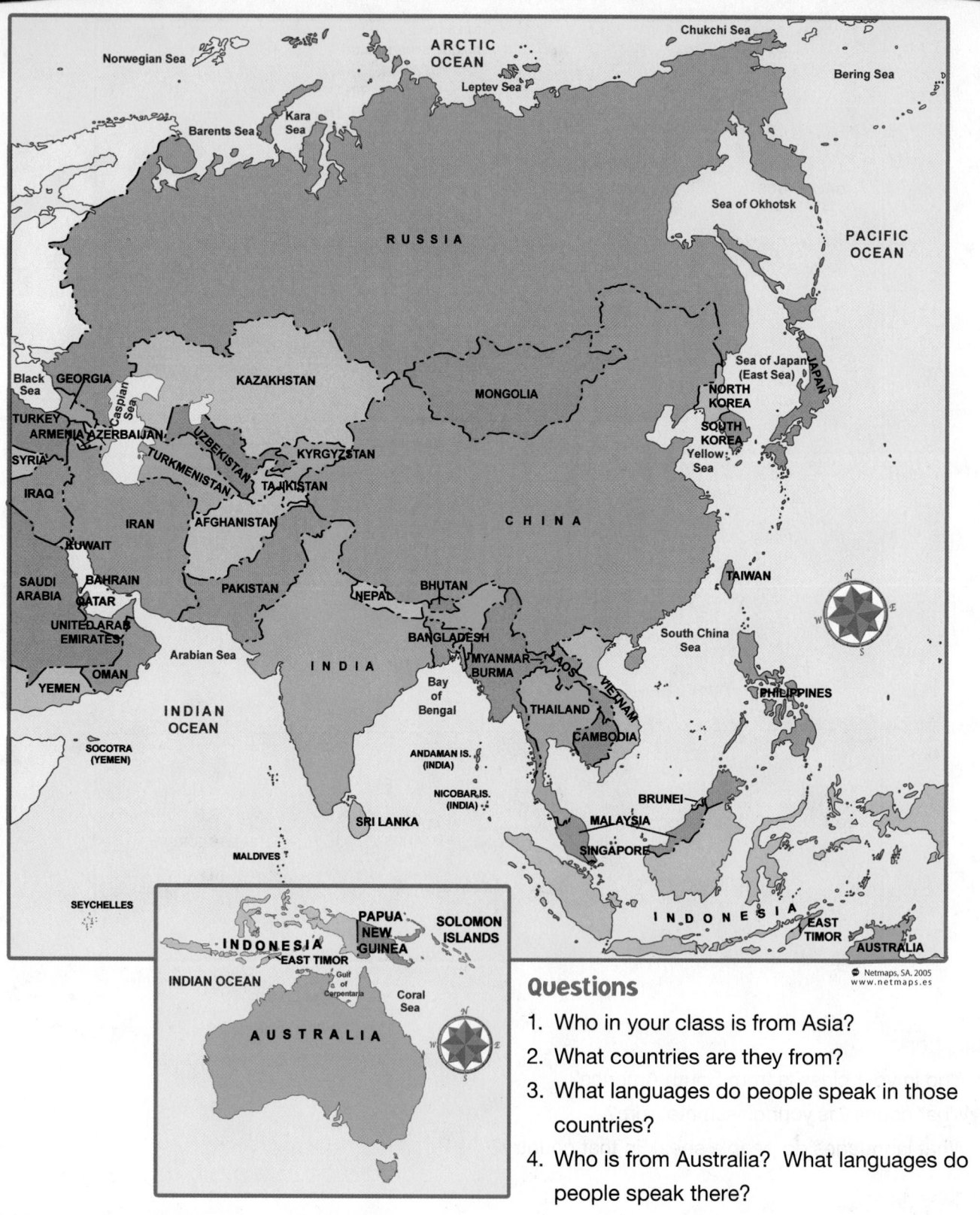

Questions

1. Who in your class is from Asia?
2. What countries are they from?
3. What languages do people speak in those countries?
4. Who is from Australia? What languages do people speak there?

Map of Europe, Africa, and the Middle East

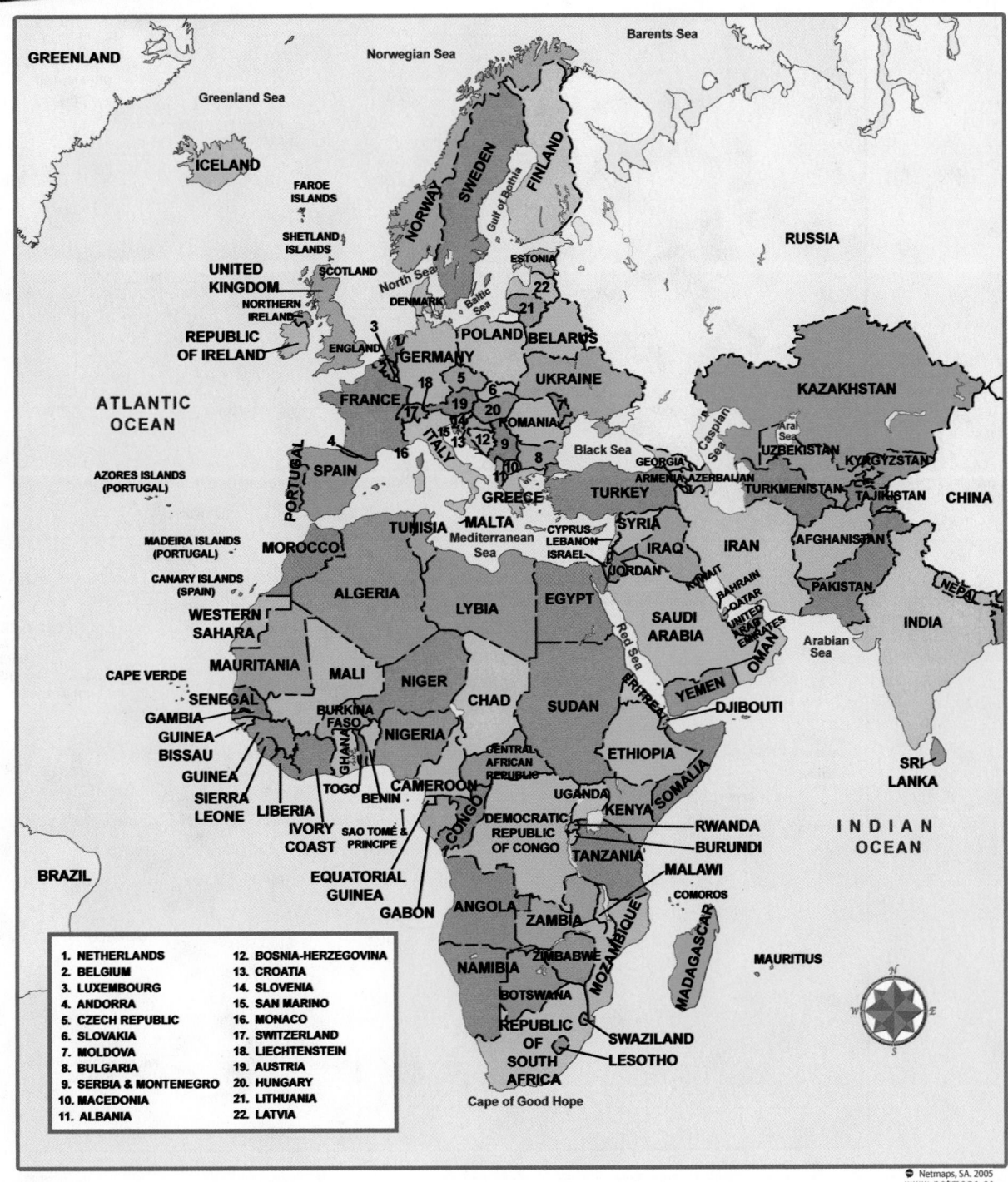

1. NETHERLANDS
2. BELGIUM
3. LUXEMBOURG
4. ANDORRA
5. CZECH REPUBLIC
6. SLOVAKIA
7. MOLDOVA
8. BULGARIA
9. SERBIA & MONTENEGRO
10. MACEDONIA
11. ALBANIA
12. BOSNIA-HERZEGOVINA
13. CROATIA
14. SLOVENIA
15. SAN MARINO
16. MONACO
17. SWITZERLAND
18. LIECHTENSTEIN
19. AUSTRIA
20. HUNGARY
21. LITHUANIA
22. LATVIA

Questions

1. Who in your class is from Europe? Africa? The Middle East?

2. What countries are your classmates from?

3. What languages do people speak in those countries?

Map of the World

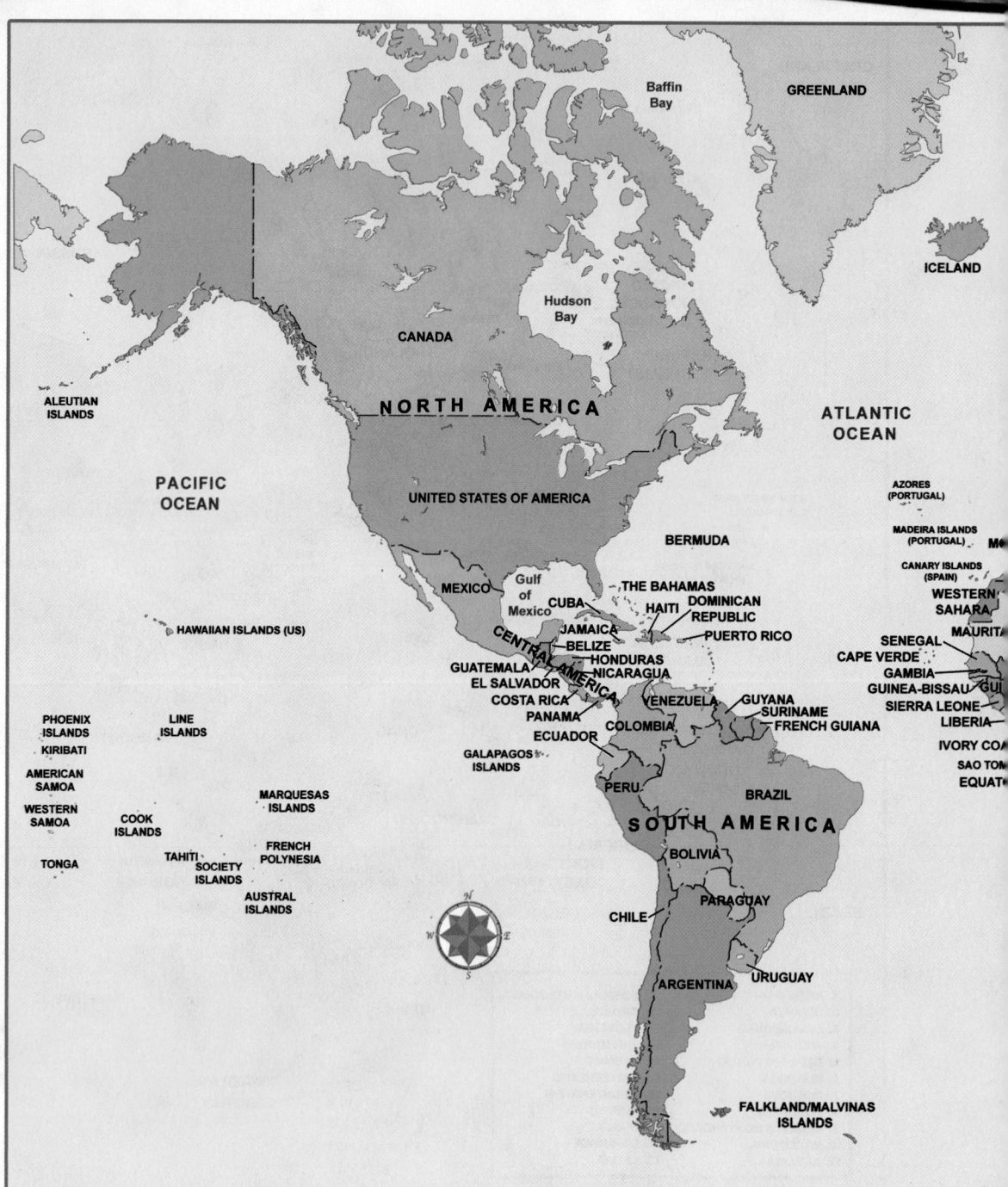

Baffin Bay

GREENLAND

ICELAND

Hudson Bay

CANADA

ALEUTIAN ISLANDS

NORTH AMERICA

ATLANTIC OCEAN

PACIFIC OCEAN

UNITED STATES OF AMERICA

AZORES (PORTUGAL)

MADEIRA ISLANDS (PORTUGAL)

BERMUDA

CANARY ISLANDS (SPAIN)

MEXICO

Gulf of Mexico

CUBA

THE BAHAMAS

DOMINICAN REPUBLIC

HAITI

WESTERN SAHARA

JAMAICA

BELIZE

PUERTO RICO

MAURITA

HAWAIIAN ISLANDS (US)

CENTRAL AMERICA

HONDURAS

SENEGAL

CAPE VERDE

GUATEMALA

NICARAGUA

GAMBIA

EL SALVADOR

COSTA RICA

GUINEA-BISSAU

GUI

PANAMA

VENEZUELA

GUYANA

SIERRA LEONE

LIBERIA

PHOENIX ISLANDS

LINE ISLANDS

COLOMBIA

SURINAME

FRENCH GUIANA

IVORY COA

KIRIBATI

ECUADOR

SAO TOM

GALAPAGOS ISLANDS

EQUAT

AMERICAN SAMOA

MARQUESAS ISLANDS

PERU

BRAZIL

WESTERN SAMOA

COOK ISLANDS

SOUTH AMERICA

TONGA

TAHITI

SOCIETY ISLANDS

FRENCH POLYNESIA

BOLIVIA

AUSTRAL ISLANDS

PARAGUAY

CHILE

ARGENTINA

URUGUAY

FALKLAND/MALVINAS ISLANDS

Questions

1. Where are you now on this map?

2. Where is your country?

3. Where is your teacher's country?

4. Where is your partner's country?

ARCTIC OCEAN

Barents Sea

RUSSIA

Bering Sea

Sea of Okhotsk

EUROPE

ASIA

PACIFIC OCEAN

KAZAKHSTAN

MONGOLIA

Black Sea
GEORGIA
ARMENIA
AZERBAIJAN
Caspian Sea
UZBEKISTAN
KYRGYZSTAN
TAJIKISTAN

NORTH KOREA
Sea of Japan
SOUTH KOREA
JAPAN

TURKEY
TURKMENISTAN
CHINA
East China Sea

Mediterranean Sea
CYPRUS
LEBANON
ISRAEL
SYRIA
JORDAN
IRAQ
KUWAIT
IRAN
AFGHANISTAN
BAHRAIN
PAKISTAN
NEPAL
BHUTAN

TUNISIA

WAKE ISLAND (US)

LIBYA
EGYPT
QATAR
SAUDI ARABIA
UNITED ARAB EMIRATES
INDIA
MYANMAR
BURMA
TAIWAN

NORTHERN MARIANA ISLANDS

AFRICA
ERITREA
YEMEN
OMAN
Arabian Sea
LAOS
VIETNAM
GUAM

NIGER
CHAD
SUDAN
DJIBOUTI
SOCOTRA (YEMEN)
BANGLADESH
THAILAND
South China Sea
PHILIPPINES

MARSHALL ISLANDS

CENTRAL AFRICAN REPUBLIC
ETHIOPIA
SOMALIA
SRI LANKA
CAMBODIA
YAP
PALAU

CAMEROON

FEDERATED STATES OF MICRONESIA

NIGERIA
UGANDA
KENYA
BRUNEI
MALAYSIA
SINGAPORE
NAURU

CONGO
DEMOCRATIC REPUBLIC OF CONGO
RWANDA
BURUNDI
TANZANIA
MALAWI
COMOROS
INDIAN OCEAN
INDONESIA
PAPUA NEW GUINEA
SOLOMON ISLANDS
TUVALU

ANGOLA
ZAMBIA
EAST TIMOR

ZIMBABWE
MADAGASCAR
MAURITIUS
Coral Sea
VANUATU
FIJI

NAMIBIA
BOTSWANA
MOZAMBIQUE
REUNION (FRANCE)
NEW CALEDONIA

REPUBLIC OF SOUTH AFRICA
SWAZILAND
LESOTHO
AUSTRALIA

ATLANTIC OCEAN
TASMANIA (Australia)
NEW ZEALAND

ICELAND
FAROE ISLANDS
NORWAY
SWEDEN
Gulf of Bothnia
FINLAND

SHETLAND ISLANDS

SCOTLAND
North Sea
ESTONIA

UNITED KINGDOM
NETHERLANDS
LUXEMBURG
BELGIUM
DENMARK
Baltic Sea
LATVIA
RUSSIA

NORTHERN IRELAND
LITHUANIA

REPUBLIC OF IRELAND
ENGLAND
GERMANY
POLAND
BELARUS

EUROPE
CZECH REPUBLIC
UKRAINE
LIECHTENSTEIN
SLOVAKIA

FRANCE
AUSTRIA
HUNGARY
MOLDOVA

G. Gascogne
SLOVENIA
CROATIA
ROMANIA

MONACO
SAN MARINO
BOSNIA-H.
SERBIA & MONTENEGRO

ANDORRA
ITALY
BULGARIA

PORTUGAL
SPAIN
SWITZERLAND
MACEDONIA
ALBANIA
TURKEY

GREECE

MALTA

Nations and Nationalities

NATIONS	NATIONALITIES	NATIONS	NATIONALITIES
Afghanistan	Afghani	Lebanon	Lebanese
Albania	Albanian	Liberia	Liberian
Algeria	Algerian	Libya	Libyan
Angola	Angolan	Lithuania	Lithuanian
Argentina	Argentinian	Mexico	Mexican
Australia	Australian	Mongolia	Mongolian
Bolivia	Bolivian	Morocco	Moroccan
Brazil	Brazilian	Namibia	Namibian
Bulgaria	Bulgarian	The Netherlands	Dutch
Burma	Burmese	Nicaragua	Nicaraguan
Canada	Canadian	Nigeria	Nigerian
Chile	Chilean	Norway	Norwegian
China	Chinese	Pakistan	Pakistani
Costa Rica	Costa Rican	Panama	Panamanian
Cuba	Cuban	Peru	Peruvian
Denmark	Danish	Philippines	Philippino
The Dominican	Dominican	Poland	Polish
Republic		Portugal	Portuguese
Ecuador	Ecuadorian	Romania	Romanian
Egypt	Egyptian	Russia	Russian
England (U.K.)	English	Saudi Arabia	Saudi
Eritrea	Eritrean	Scotland (U.K.)	Scottish
Estonia	Estonian	Senegal	Senegalese
Ethiopia	Ethiopian	Somalia	Somali
Haiti	Haitian	South Africa	South African
Finland	Finnish	Spain	Spanish
France	French	Sudan	Sudanese
Georgia	Georgian	Sweden	Swedish
Germany	German	Switzerland	Swiss
Greece	Greek	Syria	Syrian
Guatemala	Guatemalan	Taiwan	Taiwanese
Hungary	Hungarian	Thailand	Thai
Iceland	Icelandic	Tunisia	Tunisian
India	Indian	Turkey	Turkish
Indonesia	Indonesian	Uganda	Ugandan
Iraq	Iraqi	Ukraine	Ukrainian
Iran	Iranian	United States of	American
Ireland	Irish	America	
Israel	Israeli	Vietnam	Vietnamese
Italy	Italian	Venezuela	Venezuelan
Japan	Japanese	Yemen	Yemeni
Kenya	Kenyan	Yugoslavia	Yugoslavian
Korea	Korean	Zambia	Zambian
Kuwait	Kuwaiti		

Questions

1. Where are you from?
2. What's your nationality?

Numbers

CARDINAL NUMBERS

1 one	18 eighteen	80 eighty
2 two	19 nineteen	90 ninety
3 three	20 twenty	100 one hundred
4 four	21 twenty-one	101 one hundred one
5 five	22 twenty-two	102 one hundred two
6 six	23 twenty-three	200 two hundred
7 seven	24 twenty-four	300 three hundred
8 eight	25 twenty-five	400 four hundred
9 nine	26 twenty-six	500 five hundred
10 ten	27 twenty-seven	1,000 one thousand
11 eleven	28 twenty-eight	2,000 two thousand
12 twelve	29 twenty-nine	10,000 ten thousand
13 thirteen	30 thirty	100,000 one hundred thousand
14 fourteen	40 forty	1,000,000 one million
15 fifteen	50 fifty	10, 000,000 ten million
16 sixteen	60 sixty	100,000,000 one hundred million
17 seventeen	70 seventy	1,000,000,000 one billion

ORDINAL NUMBERS

1st first	21st twenty-first
2nd second	22nd twenty-second
3rd third	23rd twenty-third
4th fourth	24th twenty-fourth
5th fifth	25th twenty-fifth
6th sixth	26th twenty-sixth
7th seventh	27th twenty-seventh
8th eighth	28th twenty-eighth
9th ninth	29th twenty-ninth
10th tenth	30th thirtieth
11th eleventh	40th fortieth
12th twelfth	50th fiftieth
13th thirteenth	60th sixtieth
14th fourteenth	70th seventieth
15th fifteenth	80th eightieth
16th sixteenth	90th ninetieth
17th seventh	100th one hundredth
18th eighteenth	1,000th one thousandth
19th nineteenth	
20th twentieth	

Address Abbrevations

TITLES	
Atty.	Attorney
Dr.	Doctor
Jr.	Junior
Miss	Miss
Mr.	Mister
Mrs.	"Missus" (married woman)
Ms.	"Miz"
Prof.	Professor

STREET ADDRESS	
Apt.	Apartment
Ave.	Avenue
Blvd.	Boulevard
Ct.	Court
Dr.	Drive
Hwy.	Highway
Ln.	Lane
No.	Number
Pl.	Place
Rd.	Road
St.	Street
Ter.	Terrace
Wy.	Way

U.S.A. STATES					
AL	Alabama	MD	Maryland	RI	Rhode Island
AK	Alaska	MA	Massachusetts	SC	South Carolina
AZ	Arizona	MI	Michigan	SD	South Dakota
AR	Arkansas	MN	Minnesota	TN	Tennessee
CA	California	MS	Mississippi	TX	Texas
CO	Colorado	MO	Missouri	UT	Utah
CT	Connecticut	MT	Montana	VT	Vermont
DE	Delaware	NE	Nebraska	VA	Virginia
FL	Florida	NV	Nevada	WA	Washington
GA	Georgia	NH	New Hampshire	WV	West Virginia
HI	Hawaii	NJ	New Jersey	WI	Wisconsin
IL	Illinois	NM	New Mexico	WY	Wyoming
ID	Idaho	NY	New York		
IN	Indiana	NC	North Carolina		
IA	Iowa	ND	North Dakota		
KS	Kansas	OH	Ohio		
KY	Kentucky	OK	Oklahoma		
LA	Louisiana	OR	Oregon		
ME	Maine	PA	Pennsylvania		

Inside the Body

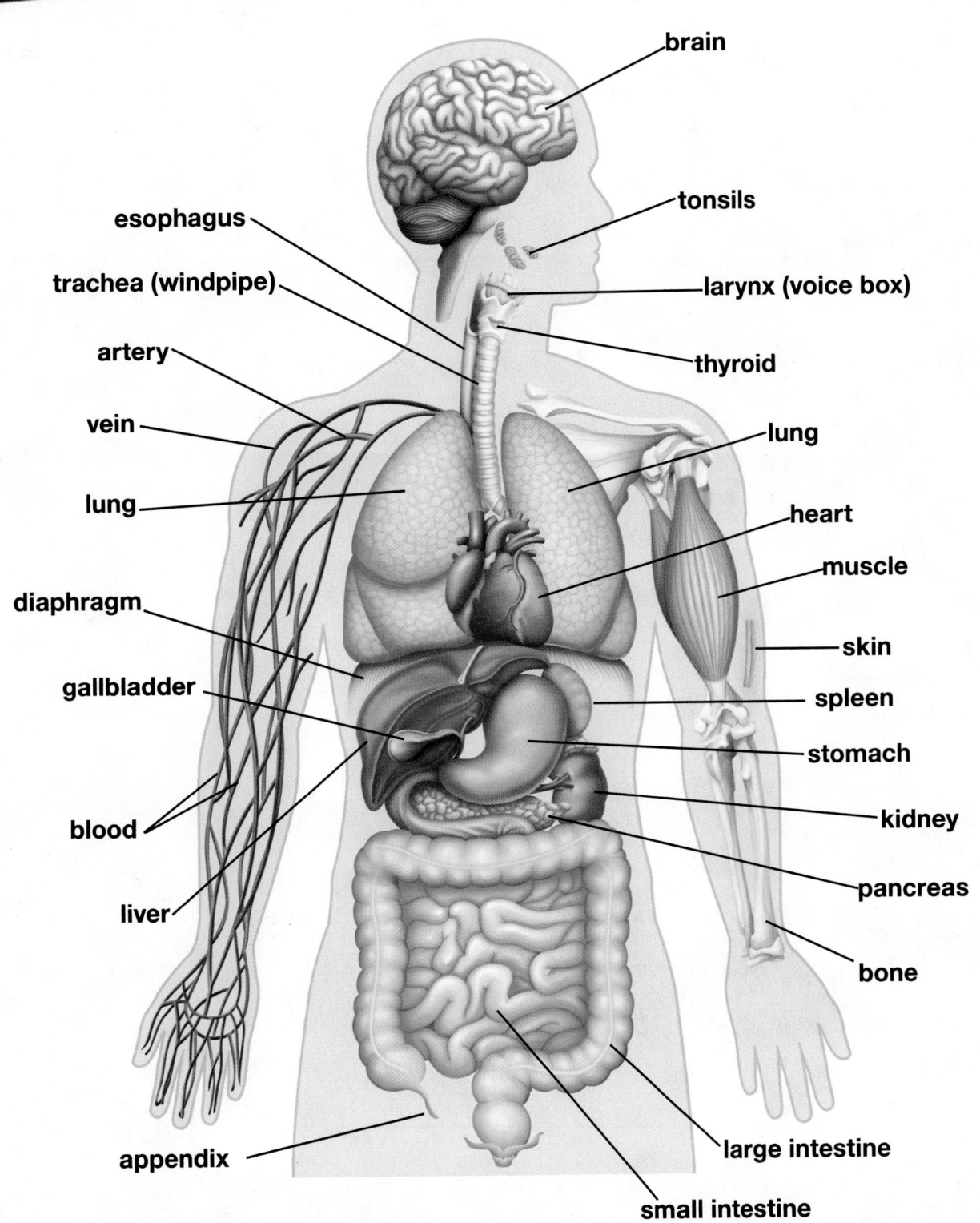

brain

esophagus

trachea (windpipe)

artery

vein

lung

diaphragm

gallbladder

blood

liver

appendix

tonsils

larynx (voice box)

thyroid

lung

heart

muscle

skin

spleen

stomach

kidney

pancreas

bone

large intestine

small intestine

Audioscript

UNIT 1 WELCOME TO CLASS!
Listening Practice
1. What do you hear?
1. What's his name?
2. What's she doing?
3. Where are you from?
4. What color is that shirt?
5. Blue is my favorite color.
6. What are you drinking?
7. I'm so sad!
8. Don't wear your gray T-shirt.

2. Questions and answers
1. What's that?
2. What are you and your friend doing?
3. How are you today?
4. Why is Jose yawning?
5. What color is the teacher's dress?
6. Where's my pen?
7. What's her name?
8. Where's France?

3. About you
1. What are you wearing today?
2. What is your teacher doing now?
3. What's on your desk?

Assessment Part 3: Listening
1. Hi. How are you?
2. What are you wearing?
3. Where are you from?
4. What color is that?
5. Where is the teacher?
6. What are you doing?

UNIT 2 EVERYDAY LIFE
Listening Practice
1. What do you hear?
1. When do you sleep?
2. Is that your brother?
3. This is my wife.
4. I leave for work at 7:50.
5. Is it 8:30 now?
6. She gets up at 6:14.
7. What does he do fifth?
8. Does she do housework?
9. Is that Area Code 212?

2. Questions and answers
1. How often is he late to class?
2. Does she take a shower every day?
3. How many cousins do you have?
4. Do you brush your teeth before breakfast?
5. What is she doing in the picture?

6. Do you do homework on weekends?
7. What time do you go to bed at night?
8. How old is your uncle?
9. What does she do every day?
10. Is he feeding the baby in the picture?

3. How about you?
1. Are you an early bird or a night owl?
2. Are you from a big family or a small family?
3. What time does your English class start and end?
4. Does your best friend have a phone?

Assessment Part 3: Listening
1. Does she make her bed every day?
2. What do they do on weekends?
3. How old is your sister?
4. What does he do first every morning?
5. How often do you do the dishes?
6. What do you do after class?

UNIT 3 YOUR HOME
Listening Practice
1. What do you hear?
1. Please don't park the car in the garage.
2. Her apartment number is 7J.
3. Our address is 25 Main Street.
4. The zip code is 85469.
5. The new apartment building has 13 stories.
6. Please set the table.
7. What do you have to do today?
8. The kids' bedroom is really messy.

2. Questions and answers
1. Is your bedroom messy?
2. Are these dishes dirty or clean?
3. What does she have to do today?
4. Is there a dishwasher in your kitchen?
5. Do you have to do homework today?
6. Where do you do laundry?
7. What's Rosa's address?
8. Where do you keep your pajamas?
9. These dishes are really pretty.
10. Why are you putting that mousetrap in the kitchen?

3. About you
1. What's your address?
2. Is your room usually neat or messy?
3. What do you have to do today?
4. What do you want to do this weekend?

1. What do you call this in English?
2. Do you live in a house?
3. Where are my slippers?
4. Why are you calling the plumber?
5. Is your bedroom neat?
6. Where do you watch TV?

UNIT 4 FOOD

Listening Practice

1. **What do they need?**

   CONVERSATION 1

   A: Let's make a fruit salad!
   B: Good idea. Do we need anything from the supermarket?
   A: Well, we have peaches and oranges in the refrigerator.
   B: OK. So what do we need?
   A: Bananas, strawberries, and . . . grapes.
   B: Bananas, strawberries, and grapes. Anything else?
   A: No, we're all set.
   B: OK! Let's go!

   CONVERSATION 2

   A: Let's make chicken vegetable soup!
   B: Great idea. Do we need anything from the supermarket?
   A: Well, we have chicken and we have onions.
   B: OK. Do we have any other vegetables?
   A: No. We need carrots, celery, and potatoes.
   B: Carrots, celery, and potatoes? Anything else?
   A: Yes, we also need green beans.
   B: OK! Let's go!

2. **At the supermarket**

   CONVERSATION 1

   CUSTOMER: Excuse me. Where can I find the canned goods?
   STOCK CLERK: Canned goods? Hmm. They're in Aisle 2.
   CUSTOMER: Thanks.

   CONVERSATION 2

   CUSTOMER: Excuse me. Where can I find the frozen foods?
   STOCK CLERK: The frozen foods? They're in Aisle 1.
   CUSTOMER: All right. Thank you.

   CONVERSATION 3

   CUSTOMER: Excuse me. Where can I find rice?
   STOCK CLERK: Rice? That's in Dry Goods. That's Aisle 3.
   CUSTOMER: OK. Thanks.

3. **Meals**

   CONVERSATION 1

   MALE: Would you like some more coffee?
   FEMALE: No, thanks. I'm all set.
   MALE: How about a piece of toast?
   FEMALE: Yes, please. I'm hungry this morning!

CONVERSATION 2

MALE: Please pass me the beans.
FEMALE: Here you are.
MALE: Thanks.
FEMALE: Would you like some more pork or rice?
MALE: No, thanks. I'm not very hungry tonight.

CONVERSATION 3

MALE: What is your lunch special today?
FEMALE: Half a chicken salad sandwich and a bowl of soup.
MALE: What are your soups today?
FEMALE: We have vegetable soup and broccoli soup.
MALE: I'll have the lunch special with broccoli soup.
FEMALE: Coming right up!

CONVERSATION 4

MALE: May I help you?
FEMALE: I'd like a hamburger and French fries, please.
MALE: OK. One hamburger and some fries. Anything else?
FEMALE: No, thanks. I'm all set.

Assessment Part 3: Listening

1. Where can I find the ice cream?
2. Anything else?
3. What's your lunch special today?
4. Where can I find fresh shellfish?
5. Would you like some more rice?
6. May I help you?
7. What are healthy breakfast foods?
8. What's your favorite fruit?

UNIT 5 YOUR COMMUNITY

Listening Practice

1. **May I help you?**

   CLERK: May I help you?
   CUSTOMER: Yes, I'd like to mail this package to Chicago.
   CLERK: How do you want to send it?
   CUSTOMER: Priority. Tell me, how long does it take to get there?
   CLERK: About three days.

2. **911**

   OPERATOR: 911. This call is being recorded. What's the emergency?
   WOMAN: There's a fire in the apartment building across the street.
   OPERATOR: Where are you calling from? What's your address?
   WOMAN: I'm calling from 167 Main Street.
   OPERATOR: What's happening now?
   WOMAN: There's smoke coming out of a window.
   OPERATOR: Is anyone in the apartment building?
   WOMAN: I don't know.
   OPERATOR: OK. The fire truck and ambulance are on the way.

3. **Where is it?**

CONVERSATION 1

MAN: Excuse me. Where is the movie theater?

WOMAN: It's on Main Street.

MAN: How do I get there?

WOMAN: Go straight. Take a right on Main Street. Go past the library. The movie theater is on the left.

MAN: Take a right on Main Street. Go past the library and it's on the left?

WOMAN: That's right.

MAN: Thank you.

CONVERSATION 2

MAN: Excuse me. Where's the drugstore?

WOMAN: It's on the corner of James Avenue and Main Street.

MAN: How do I get there?

WOMAN: Go straight. Go past the laundromat, and the drugstore is on the left.

MAN: Go straight. Go past the laundromat and it's on the left?

WOMAN: Uh-huh.

CONVERSATION 3

MAN: Excuse me. Where is the school?

WOMAN: It's on Main Street. It's across the street from the bank.

MAN: How do I get there?

WOMAN: Go straight. At the traffic light, take a left on Main Street. The school is on the right.

MAN: Go straight. Take a left on Main Street and the school is on the left?

WOMAN: No. The school is on the right, after the playground.

MAN: Oh, it's on the right, after the playground. OK. Thank you.

Assessment Part 3: Listening

1. How long does it take to get there?
2. How do I get to the library?
3. May I help you?
4. Where is the movie theater?
5. 911. What's the emergency?
6. How do you want to send it?

UNIT 6 SHOPPING

Listening Practice

1. **Questions and answers**

1. Can I help you?
2. How much are they?
3. What size do you wear?
4. How do they fit?
5. What's the item number?
6. How would you like to pay?
7. How much is shipping?
8. Can I help you?

2. **Where are they?**

CONVERSATION 1

SALESCLERK: Can I help you?

CUSTOMER: Yes. I like that ring. Can I try it on?

SALESCLERK: Certainly. The silver one or the gold one?

CUSTOMER: The silver one, please.

CONVERSATION 2

CUSTOMER: I like this dress. Can I try it on?

SALESCLERK: Of course! The fitting rooms are over there, next to the sweaters.

CONVERSATION 3

SHOPPER: Where can I get a nice scarf?

SALESCLERK: Hmmm. Try the boutique on level 1. It's next to the coffee shop.

SHOPPER: OK. Thank you!

CONVERSATION 4

MAN: What a good deal! That watch is only $10. And it's gold!

WOMAN: Wow! How much is shipping?

MAN: Only $5.00! But I have to call now because they only have six left.

WOMAN: Hurry! Here's the phone.

3. **Placing an order**

1. Can I help you?
2. What's the item number?
3. What color do you want?
4. What size?
5. How would you like to pay?
6. What is the card number and expiration date?

Assessment Part 3: Listening

1. How much is it?
2. Can I try them on?
3. What size do you wear?
4. What's the expiration date?
5. Can I help you?
6. How does it fit?
7. How would you like to pay?
8. Where can I get a pair of slippers?

UNIT 7 YOUR CALENDAR

Listening Practice

1. **Holidays**

CONVERSATION 1 (doorbell rings and door opens)

CHILDREN: Trick or treat!

WOMAN: Well, hi there! Look at these terrific costumes. Here you go, kids. Take some candy.

CONVERSATION 2

WOMAN: Oh, chocolates! Thanks, sweetie!

MAN: You're welcome. I love you.

WOMAN: I love you, too.

CONVERSATION 3

MAN: We took Marty and Joanie to Tracy's Department Store yesterday to see Santa Claus. They thought that was great!

WOMAN: And they were really surprised to find so many presents under the tree this morning. This is such a fun holiday for children!

2. A weather report

WEATHERPERSON: Across the nation today, we have a high temperature of 88° in Florida and a low of 19° in Montana. The weather tomorrow will be sunny and hot in the Southeast, cold in the North, and rainy in the West. And what kind of weather are we looking at for our area? Well, the weather here will be cloudy and cool, with a high of 56°.

3. Where are they?

CONVERSATION 1

WOMAN: What a beautiful day for the beach!

MAN: Yes, it is. And it's a great day to play volleyball. I think I'll join the game.

CONVERSATION 2

WOMAN: Johnny! Stop playing in the rain! Come over here under the umbrella. You're getting all wet.

CONVERSATION 3

WOMAN: (calling loudly) Honey, do you want your cap? It's cold.

MAN: That's OK. I'm fine. I'm wearing my earmuffs.

Assessment Part 3: Listening

1. Oh, no! Is it raining?
2. When is Thanksgiving this year?
3. When were you born?
4. Are you going to take a vacation this summer?
5. What's today's date? Do you know?
6. Why are you packing your bathing suit?

UNIT 8 YOUR HEALTH

Listening Practice

1. How are you doing?

FEMALE: How are you doing?

MALE: Not so well.

FEMALE: What's the matter?

MALE: I have a bad headache.

FEMALE: A headache? I'm sorry to hear that.

MALE: Thanks. Hey, what medicine do you recommend for headaches?

FEMALE: Try Linux aspirin. It really works.

MALE: Linux aspirin . . . OK. Thanks!

2. Making an appointment

CONVERSATION 1

RECEPTIONIST: Good morning. Doctor Lander's General Practice. May I help you?

FEMALE PATIENT: Yes, please. This is Lynn Weber. I'd like to make an appointment with Dr. Lander.

RECEPTIONIST: What's the reason for the appointment?

FEMALE PATIENT: My allergies are terrible.

RECEPTIONIST: How about tomorrow at 9:00?

FEMALE PATIENT: Thursday at 9:00? OK.

CONVERSATION 2

RECEPTIONIST: Good morning. Doctor Lander's General Practice. May I help you?

MALE PATIENT: Yes, I'd like to make an appointment with Dr. Lander.

RECEPTIONIST: Your name, please?

MALE PATIENT: Tom Mitchell.

RECEPTIONIST: What's the reason for the appointment?

MALE PATIENT: I feel terrible. I have a fever, a headache, and a stiff neck.

RECEPTIONIST: Hmmm . . . a fever, a headache, and a stiff neck? Can you come in this morning, Mr. Mitchell—at 9:20?

MALE PATIENT: At 9:20? OK. I'm on my way.

CONVERSATION 3

RECEPTIONIST: Good morning. Doctor Lander's General Practice. May I help you?

FEMALE PATIENT: Yes, I'd like to make an appointment with Dr. Lander. My name is Anita Maxwell.

RECEPTIONIST: What's the reason for the appointment?

FEMALE PATIENT: I have a cold and a sore throat.

RECEPTIONIST: Do you have a fever?

FEMALE PATIENT: No, I don't.

RECEPTIONIST: How about 9:20 tomorrow morning?

FEMALE PATIENT: 9:20 on Thursday? OK.

3. Follow the signs!

1. Help! I need to see a doctor right now. I have a terrible stomachache.
2. Hello. I need to check in. I'm here for a two-day stay.
3. Hi. I'm here for a 2:15 appointment with Dr. Mainz.
4. How do I get to the fourth floor?
5. Where can I get a cup of coffee?

1. What's the matter?
2. What time is your appointment?
3. I have a bad toothache.
4. What's the reason for your appointment?
5. Where's Dr. Payson's office?
6. What are the visiting hours?
7. What medicine do you recommend for a fever?
8. I feel great. My cold finally went away.
9. What are three healthy habits?
10. Can I see your insurance card?

UNIT 9 YOUR WORK

Listening Practice

1. **I'm calling about the job.**

EMPLOYER: Kitchens and Bathrooms Are Us. May I help you?

APPLICANT: Yes. My name is Jim Jones. I'm calling about your ad in the paper for a carpenter.

EMPLOYER: Yes, we're looking for an experienced carpenter. You have to have your own transportation and tools.

APPLICANT: That's fine.

EMPLOYER: Can you come in for an interview this afternoon, Jim?

APPLICANT: This afternoon? Yes, that would be fine. What time?

EMPLOYER: How's 4:00?

APPLICANT: That's OK. Thank you very much.

EMPLOYER: You're welcome. See you then.

2. **What do you do?**

ANNIE: What do you do, Michael?

MICHAEL: Well, I was a police officer for twenty years, but now I'm a security guard. I just started a new job at First National Bank. What about you, Annie?

ANNIE: I'm a fourth-grader teacher.

MICHAEL: Oh, so you work during the day.

ANNIE: Do you work at night?

MICHAEL: Yes. I work the third shift. And I love it. It's really quiet.

ANNIE: I love my job, too. I guess we're lucky, Michael. A lot of people aren't happy with their jobs.

3. **Questions and answers**

1. What do you do?
2. What would you like to do in the future?
3. Who pays for the employees' uniforms?
4. What hours do you work?
5. Why is Ms. Sato so happy?
6. How do you like working the first shift?
7. Do you work full time?
8. Why was Jorge laid off?

1. Why are you changing jobs?
2. Do you like working the second shift?
3. Why are you looking for a job in a bank?
4. What was your last job?
5. Why do you like your job?

UNIT 10 YOUR FREE TIME

Listening Practice

1. **What do they like to do in their free time?**

JIM: What do you like to do in your free time, Alice?

ALICE: Well, I love to play sports. I like to go camping, and I like to have picnics in the park. What about you?

JIM: Well, I don't really like sports, camping, or going to the park. I like to go to art museums and the theater.

ALICE: Hmmm. Art museums? The theater? Not me! How about movies? Do you like to go to movies?

JIM: Yes, I do! I love to go to the movies.

ALICE: I do too! And do you like to watch TV?

JIM: I like to watch game shows.

ALICE: I do too. So, we both like to go to the movies and to watch game shows on TV.

JIM: Yep. So I won't invite you to a museum or the theater.

ALICE: And I won't invite you to play sports, to go camping, or to go to the park!

2. **Going out**

A: Would you like to go to a concert with me on Sunday night?

B: Sure! What concert?

A: The Play Monkeys.

B: I love the Play Monkeys! I like to dance to their music! What time?

A: 8:00.

B: OK! 8:00 on Sunday. I'll be there!

3. **About you**

1. How often do you go to the library?
2. What do you like to do in your free time?
3. What are your favorite TV shows?
4. What kinds of movies do you like?
5. What's your favorite sport?
6. Do you like to play Frisbee?
7. What is your plan for learning more English?

Assessment Part 3: Listening

1. Would you like to go to the theater with me?
2. How often do you exercise?
3. What do you like to do in your free time?
4. What kinds of movies do you like?
5. What can you borrow from the library?
6. What's your favorite sport to watch on TV?
7. What times are the shows?
8. I like cartoons.

Answer Key

UNIT 1 WELCOME TO CLASS!
Lesson 1: Introductions
1. a. 3   b. 2   c. 1   d. 4   e. 5

Lesson 2: Countries
1. a. 6   b. 8   c. 4   d. 9
   e. 5   f. 7   g. 2   h. 1
   i. 3

Lesson 3: Feelings
1. a. 6   b. 3   c. 4   d. 5
   e. 1   f. 7   g. 2   h. 9   i. 8

Lesson 4: Clothes and Colors
1. a. 2   b. 5   c. 4   d. 7   e. 6
   f. 3   g. 1   h. 8   i. 9   j. 13
   k. 12   l. 10   m. 11

Lesson 5: In Your Classroom
1. a. 6   b. 14   c. 12   d. 3   e. 8
   f. 11   g. 9   h. 2   i. 7   j. 1
   k. 15   l. 5   m. 4   n. 13   o. 10

Lesson 6: Taking a Break
1. a. 6   b. 12   c. 3   d. 9   e. 2
   f. 8 g. 10 h. 7 i. 4 j. 14
   k. 1   l. 5   m. 13   n. 11

Listening Practice
1. 1. b   2. b   3. b   4. a
   5. a   6. b   7. a   8. b

2. 1. a   2. a   3. a   4. b
   5. a   6. b   7. b   8. a

Assessment Part 3
1. b   2. a   3. a
4. b   5. b   6. b

UNIT 2 EVERYDAY LIFE
Lesson 1: Your Family
1. a. 7, 11 b. 11   c. 9, 10, 11 d. 8
   e. 4   f. 8, 10 g. 2, 4   h. 3, 6
   i. 5   j. 6   k. 10, 8   l. 7   m. 1, 5

5. a. 4   b. 10   c. 8   d. 9   e. 2
   f. 1   g. 3   h. 7   i. 6   j. 5

Lesson 2: Time
1. a. 3   b. 5   c. 8   d. 4
   e. 2   f. 1   g. 6   h. 7

Lesson 3: Morning Routines
1. a. 8th   b. 4th   c. 6th   d. 1st
   e. 7th   f. 9th   g. 5th   h. 7th
   i. 2nd   j. 3rd   k. 7th

Lesson 4: Housework
1. a. 7   b. 3   c. 4   d. 6
   e. 2   f. 9   g. 8   h. 1   i. 5

Lesson 5: Everyday Life
1. a. 6   b. 1   c. 4   d. 3
   e. 5   f. 7   g. 8   h. 2

Lesson 6: Telephone Calls
1. a. 5   b. 1   c. 2   d. 8
   e. 3   f. 4   g. 6   h. 7

Listening Practice
1. 1. b   2. b   3. a   4. b
   5. a   6. a   7. b   8. b   9. a

2. 1. a   2. b   3. a   4. a
   5. b   6. a   7. b   8. b
   9. a   10. a

Assessment Part 3
1. b   2. b   3. a   4. b
5. a   6. a

UNIT 3 YOUR HOME
Lesson 1: Homes
1. a. 1   b. 11   c. 10   d. 6
   e. 4   f. 8   g. 5   h. 2
   i. 3   j. 7   k. 9

Lesson 2: In the Kitchen
1. a. 3   b. 13   c. 8   d. 9
   e. 7   f. 5   g. 1   h. 6
   i. 4   j. 2   k. 10   n. 11   o. 12

Lesson 3: The Dining Area and Living Room
1. a. 5   b. 1   c. 4   d. 2
   e. 7   f. 8   g. 6   h. 3
   i. 9   l. 12   m. 11   n. 10

4. a. 2   b. 6   c. 5   d. 3
   e. 10   f. 8   g. 1   h. 4
   k. 7   l. 9

Lesson 4: Neat and Messy Bedrooms
1. a. 8   b. 3   c. 11   d. 9
   e. 6   f. 7   g. 10   h. 4
   i. 1   j. 2   k. 5

Lesson 5: The Bathroom

1. a. 1   b. 2   c. 13   d. 7
   e. 12   f. 3   g. 8   h. 11
   i. 6   j. 5   k. 9   l. 10   m. 4

Lesson 6: Problems at Home

1. a. 1   b. 7   c. 8   d. 3
   e. 2   f. 5   g. 4   h. 6
   i. 9

2. 1. c, e   2. a, f   3. b, d

Listening Practice

1. 1. a   2. a   3. b   4. a
   5. b   6. b   7. a   8. b

2. 1. b   2. a   3. a   4. b
   5. a   6. a   7. b   8. b
   9. b   10. b

Assessment Part 3

1. a   2. b   3. b   4. a
5. b   6. a

UNIT 4 FOOD

Lesson 1: Vegetables

1. a. 9   b. 8   c. 7   d. 4
   e. 10   f. 5   g. 3   h. 12
   i. 1   j. 2   k. 11   l. 6

Lesson 2: Fruit

1. a. 2   b. 11   c. 10   d. 13
   e. 8   f. 4   g. 3   h. 9
   i. 5   j. 1   k. 7   l. 6   m. 12

Lesson 3: The Supermarket

1. a. 4   b. 2   c. 11   d. 3
   e. 9   f. 6   g. 7   h. 10
   i. 8   j. 1   k. 5

Lesson 4: Breakfast

1. a. 7   b. 8   c. 3   d. 5
   e. 2   f. 10   g. 11   h. 6
   i. 9   j. 4   k. 12   l. 1

Lesson 5: Lunch

1. a. 9   b. 1   c. 3   d. 4
   e. 5   f. 8   g. 10   h. 7
   i. 2   j. 6

Lesson 6: Dinner

1. a. 7   b. 9   c. 4   d. 1
   e. 8   f. 2   g. 10   h. 5
   i. 6   j. 3

Listening Practice

1. oranges   mangos   (bananas) (grapes)
   pears   (strawberries) peaches   apples

   (carrots) (green beans) corn   (celery)
   chicken   (potatoes)   onions   green peppers

2. Aisle 1: Frozen Foods
   Aisle 2: Canned Goods
   Aisle 3: Dry Goods

3. 1. a   2. c   3. b   4. c

Assessment Part 3

1. b   2. a   3. a   4. b
5. a   6. b   7. a   8. b

UNIT 5 YOUR COMMUNITY

Lesson 1: Neighborhood and Neighbors

1. a. 6   b. 2   c. 11   d. 1
   e. 8   f. 3   g. 13   h. 5
   j. 12   k. 7   l. 10   m. 4   n. 9

Lesson 2: Around Town

1. a. 3   b. 9   c. 5   d. 8
   e. 7   f. 6   g. 11   h. 4
   i. 2   j. 10   k. 1

Lesson 3: The Post Office

1. a. 6   b. 5   c. 2   d. 1
   e. 9   f. 4   g. 7   h. 8   i. 3

Lesson 4: The Bank

1. a. 1   b. 4   c. 6   d. 5
   e. 2   f. 7   g. 3   h. 8

Lesson 5: Help! Fire!

1. a. 9   b. 10   c. 5   d. 2
   e. 12   f. 1   g. 3   h. 11
   i. 6   k. 8   l. 7   m. 4

Lesson 6: Help! Police!

1. a. 1   b. 4   c. 3   d. 2

Listening Practice

1. 1. a   2. b   3. a
2. 1. b   2. b   3. a

3.

Assessment Part 3

1. a   2. a   3. b
4. a   5. a   6. b

UNIT 6 SHOPPING

Lesson 1: Shopping at the Mall

1. a. 9   b. 13   c. 4   d. 7
   e. 8   f. 12   g. 10   h. 1
   i. 5   j. 6   k. 11   l. 3   m. 2

Lesson 2: Buying Shoes

1. a. 6   b. 9   c. 3   d. 8
   e. 11   f. 2   g. 4   h. 5
   i. 1   j. 7   k. 10

Lesson 3: Shopping for Clothing

1. a. 12   b. 14   c. 11   d. 7
   e. 10   f. 6   g. 9   h. 8   i. 4
   j. 5   k. 2   l. 3   m. 13   n. 1

3. a. 5   b. 9   c. 8   d. 3
   e. 1   f. 2   g. 10   h. 4
   i. 6   j. 7

Lesson 4: Shopping for Jewelry

1. a. 2   b. 5   c. 4   d. 7
   e. 3   f. 8   g. 6   h. 1

Lesson 5: Sales and Advertisements

1. a. 3   b. 2   c. 1   d. 4

Lesson 6: Shopping in the 21st Century

1. a. 6   b. 4   c. 1
   d. 8   e. 2   f. 7
   g. 5   h. 3   i. 9

4. 1. b   2. e   3. d   4. a   5. c

Listening Practice

1. 1. a   2. a   3. b   4. b
   5. a   6. a   7. b   8. b

2. 1. b   2. b   3. a   4. b

3. 1. Yes. I'd like to place an order.
   2. #20987.
   3. Green
   4. Extra large.
   5. With a Masterworld credit card.
   6. 2232 5545 6676 9929 and 02/11

Assessment Part 3

1. a   2. a   3. b   4. b
5. a   6. a   7. b   8. a

UNIT 7 YOUR CALENDAR

Lesson 1: Months, Years, and Birthdays

4. a. 4   b. 1   c. 5   d. 6
   e. 8   f. 9   g. 7   h. 3
   i. 10   j. 11   k. 2

Lesson 2: Dates and Holidays

1. a. 4   b. 12   c. 7   d. 9
   e. 6   f. 3   g. 1   h. 2
   i. 5   j. 11   k. 8   l. 10

3. 1. Valentine's Day   2. Halloween
   3. Thanksgiving   4. Independence Day
   5. New Year's

Lesson 3: Weather Report

1. a. 5   b. 12   c. 4   d. 10
   e. 7   f. 1   g. 6   h. 8
   i. 9   j. 3   k. 11   l. 2

3. 1. 50°F.   2. 30°C.

Lesson 4: Good and Bad Weather
1. a. 6   b. 2   c. 10   d. 8
   e. 7   f. 1   g. 12   h. 11
   i. 4   j. 3   k. 9   l. 5

2. 1. a snowy day
   2. a hailstorm
   3. a windy day
   4. a rainy day
   5. a sunny day

Lesson 5: The Seasons
1. a. 8   b. 4   c. 2   d. 3
   e. 7   f. 1   g. 5   h. 6
   i. 9   j. 10

Lesson 6: Taking a Trip
1. a. 8   b. 4   c. 3   d. 2
   e. 11   f. 5   g. 6   h. 9
   i. 1   j. 10   k. 7

Listening Practice
1. 1. b   2. c   3. b

2. 1. b   2. a   3. a   4. a

3.   2   3   1

Assessment Part 3
   1. a   2. b   3. a   4. b
   5. b   6. a

UNIT 8 YOUR HEALTH
Lesson 1: Staying Healthy
1. a. 10   b. 2   c. 6   d. 3
   e. 12   f. 8   g. 7   h. 1
   i. 5   j. 4   k. 11   l. 9

Lesson 2: What's the matter?
1. a. 9   b. 4   c. 8   d. 7
   e. 8   f. 3   g. 8   h. 1
   i. 5   j. 2   k. 6

5. 1. b   2. c   3. e   4. a   5. d

Lesson 3: The Drugstore
1. a. 5   b. 8   c. 9   d. 4
   e. 6   f. 12   g. 3   h. 11
   i. 2   j. 10   k. 7   l. 1

Lesson 4: Going to the Doctor
1. a. 5   b. 9   c. 2   d. 3
   e. 6   f. 10   g. 4   h. 7
   i. 8   j. 1

Lesson 5: Going to the Dentist
1. a. 8   b. 9   c. 2   d. 1
   e. 3   f. 10   g. 4   h. 7
   i. 5   j. 6

Lesson 6: The Hospital
1. a. 2   b. 5   c. 9   d. 4   e. 1
   f. 8   g. 6   h. 3   i. 10   j. 7

Listening Practice
1. 1. a   2. a

2. Wednesday
   9:00, Jane Smith: backache
   9:20, Tom Mitchell: fever, headache,
      stiff neck

   Thursday
   9:00, Lynn Weber: allergies
   9:20, Anita Maxwell: cold and sore throat

3.   1   5   2   4   3

Assessment Part 3
   1. a   2. b   3. a   4. a   5. a
   6. a   7. b   8. b   9. a   10. a

UNIT 9 YOUR WORK
Lesson 1: Workers and Their Work
1. a. 2   b. 10   c. 7   d. 11
   e. 5   f. 1   g. 8   h. 12
   i. 4   j. 9   k. 6   l. 3

Lesson 2: Life at Work
1. a. 3, 7   b. 2   c. 3   d. 1
   e. 6   f. 2   g. 5   h. 4
   i. 1   j. 6   k. 5   l. 1, 2 ,6, 7

Lesson 3: Looking for a Job
1. 1. d   2. a   3. g   4. k
   5. l   6. e   7. b   8. j
   9. i   10. c   11. f   12. h

Lesson 4: Job Applications

1. 1. In Greenville, Kentucky or on Marshall Rd.
    2. 734-621-4908
    3. Nurse (Surgical)
    4. Surgical Nurse at Porter Hospital
    5. High School diploma, R.N. degree
    6. Janet Wong, Donna Hunt

Lesson 5: Safety at Work

1. a. 6   b. 2   c. 5   d. 8
    e. 1   f. 4   g. 7   h. 9
    i. 10   j. 3

Lesson 6: Leaving a Job

1. a. 2, 3 b. 1   c. 3   d. 1
    e. 2   f. 3

4. a. 2   b. 2, 3 c. 3   d. 1,3
    e. 2   f. 1

Listening Practice

1. 1. b   2. a   3. b   4. a   5. a

2. 1. b   2. b   3. b   4. a   5. a

3. 1. a   2. b   3. a   4. a   5. a
    6. b   7. b   8. a

Assessment Part 3

1. 1. a   2. a   3. b   4. a   5. b

UNIT 10 YOUR FREE TIME

Lesson 1: Going Out

1. a. 9   b. 7   c. 10   d. 2
    e. 11   f. 4   g. 1   h. 6
    j. 8   k. 5   l. 3

Lesson 2: Free Time

1. a. 1   b. 9   c. 10   d. 7
    e. 5   f. 3   g. 4   h. 6
    i. 2   j. 8

Lesson 3: TV and Movies

1. a. 4   b. 5   c. 2   d. 9
    e. 6   f. 11   g. 7   h. 1
    i. 8   j. 10   k. 3

4. a. 9   b. 6   c. 4   d. 5
    e. 1   f. 3   g. 8   h. 2   i. 7

Lesson 4: The Park

1. a. 8   b. 2   c. 7   d. 1
    e. 6   f. 3   g. 5   h. 4

Lesson 5: Sports

1. a. 4   b. 7   c. 2   d. 3
    e. 5   f. 6   g. 1   h. 10
    i. 8   j. 11   k. 9

3. a. 2   b. 1   c. 4   d. 3

Lesson 6: Lifelong Learning

1. a. 7   b. 8   c. 5   d. 1
    e. 3   f. 6   g. 2   h. 9   i. 4

Listening Practice

1.

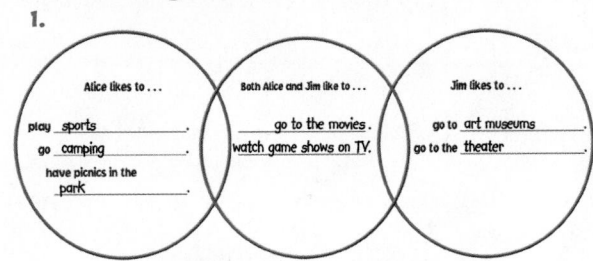

2. 1. a   2. b

Assessment Part 3

1. 1. b   2. b   3. a   4. b
    5. b   6. a   7. b   8. a

NOTES

NOTES

NOTES

NOTES

NOTES

NOTES

NOTES